The Law's Lumber Room

By

Francis Watt

Double9 BOOKS

The Law's Lumber Room
by Francis Watt

ISBN: 978-93-63059-87-0

Published by

DOUBLE 9 BOOKS
2/13-B, Ansari Road
Daryaganj, New Delhi – 110002
info@double9books.com
www.double9books.com
Tel. 011-40042856

ABOUT THE AUTHOR

Francis Watt, a meticulous legal scholar, delves into the intricacies of jurisprudence in his seminal work, "The Law's Lumber Room." Through meticulous analysis and insightful commentary, Watt navigates the labyrinthine corridors of legal theory, shedding light on the often overlooked nooks and crannies of the legal system. His magnum opus serves as a compendium of legal knowledge, offering a comprehensive exploration of the principles, precedents, and paradigms that underpin the rule of law. Within the pages of "The Law's Lumber Room," Watt masterfully dissects complex legal concepts, presenting them in a lucid and accessible manner. Drawing upon his vast expertise and erudition, he elucidates the evolution of legal thought, tracing its historical roots and examining its contemporary manifestations. From discussions on constitutional law to analyses of case law, Watt's treatise offers invaluable insights for both seasoned legal professionals and aspiring jurists. With meticulous attention to detail and a keen analytical eye, Francis Watt invites readers into the hallowed chambers of the law, where statutes come to life and legal principles take shape. "The Law's Lumber Room" stands as a testament to Watt's scholarly prowess and enduring legacy in the field of jurisprudence.

CONTENTS

PREFATORY

To the Lumber Room you drag furniture no longer fit for daily use, and there it lies, old fashioned, cumbrous, covered year by year with fresh depths of dust. Is it fanciful to apply this image to the Law? Has not that its Lumber Room of repealed Statutes, discarded methods, antiquated text-books—"many a quaint and curious volume of forgotten lore"?

But law, even when an actual part of the life of to-day is like to prove a tedious thing to the lay reader, can one hope to find the dry bones of romance in its antiquities? I venture to answer, "Yes." Among all the rubbish, the outworn instruments of cruelty, superstition, terror, there are things of interest. "Benefit of Clergy," the "Right of Sanctuary," bulk large in English literature; the "Law of the Forest" gives us a glimpse into the life of Mediæval England as actual as, though so much more sombre than, the vision conjured up in Chaucer's magic *Prologue*. "Trial by Ordeal" and "Wager of Battle" touch on superstitions and beliefs that lay at the very core of the nation's being.

"As full of fictions as English law," wrote Macaulay in the early part of the century; but we have changed that, we are more practical, if less picturesque, and John Doe and all his tribe are long out of date. Between the reign of James I. and that of Victoria all the subjects here discussed have suffered change, with one exception. The "Press-Gang" is still a legal possibility, but how hard to fancy it ever again in actual use!

I fear that these glimpses of other days may seem harsh and sombre; there is blood everywhere; the cruel consequences of law or custom are pushed to their logical conclusions with ruthless determination. The contrast to the almost morbid sentimentalism of to-day is striking. So difficult it seems to hit the just mean! But the improvement is enormous. Gibes at the Law are the solace of its victims, and no one would deprive them of so innocent a relief, yet if these cared to enquire they would often find that the mark of their jest had vanished years ago to the Lumber Room.

The plan of these papers did not permit a detailed reference to authorities, but I have mentioned every work from which I derived special assistance. I will only add that this little book originally appeared as contributions to the *National Observer* under Mr W. E. Henley's editorship. I have made a few additions and corrections.

BENEFIT OF CLERGY

"Benefit of Clergy" is a phrase which has entered into English literature and English thought. The thing itself exists no longer, though the last traces of it were only removed during the present reign; but it so strikingly illustrates certain peculiarities of English law-making, it has, moreover, so curious a history as to be interesting even to-day. It took its rise in times when the pretensions of the Church, high in themselves, were highly favoured by the secular power. The clergy was a distinct order, and to subject its members to the jurisdiction of the secular courts was deemed improper; so, when a clerk was seized under a charge of murder, or some other crime, the ordinary stepped forth and claimed him for the "Court Christian," whereto the whole matter was at once relegated. There the bishop or his deputy sat as judge. There was a jury of twelve clerks before whom the prisoner declared his innocence on oath. He was ready with twelve compurgators (a species of witnesses to character) who, after their kind, said more good of him than they had any warrant for; after which, on the question of fact, some witnesses were examined for, but none against him. This curious proceeding, which was not abolished till the time of Elizabeth, soon became a sham. Nearly every accused got off, and the rare verdict of guilty had no worse result than degradation or imprisonment.

Now, so far, the system is intelligible, but in the succeeding centuries it lost this quality. English legal reformers have ever shown a strong disinclination to make a clean sweep of a system, but they keep tinkering at it year after year with a view of making it more rational or better adapted to current needs. They did so here, and the result was a strange jumble of contradictions. First, the privilege was confined to such as had the clerical dress and tonsure, afterwards it was extended to mere assistants, the very door-keepers being held within the charmed circle; yet the line had to be drawn somewhere, and how to decide when every ruffian at his wits' end for a defence was certain with blatant voice to claim the privilege? Well, could he read? If so, ten to one he was an ecclesiastic of some sort, and therefore entitled to his clergy. And it soon came that this was the only test demanded. If you could read you were presumed a parson, and had your right to at least one crime free. As no woman could possibly be ordained, she could not "pray her clergy"—(an exception was made in the case of a professed nun)—nor might a *bigamus,* who was not a man who had committed bigamy, but one who "hath married two wives or one widow." However, a statute (1 Edw. VI., c. 12, s. 16, *temp.* 1547) made an end of this latter distinction by declaring, with quaint tautology that *bigami* were to have their clergy, "although they or any of them have been divers and sundry times married to any single woman or single women, or to any widow or widows, or to two wives or more." Before this it might well be that your chance of saving your neck depended on whether you had married a widow or not; which species was dangerous in a sense undreamt of by Mr Weller. As regards the reading, it must not be supposed that a difficult examination was passed by the prisoner before he escaped. You had but to read what came to be significantly called the Neck-verse from the book which the officer of court handed you when you "prayed your clergy." The Neck-verse was the first verse of the fifty-first Psalm in the Vulgate. It was only three words—*Miserere mei, Deus*: "Have mercy on me, O God." It seems strange that it was ever recorded of anyone that he did not read, and was therefore condemned to be hanged; for surely it were easy to get these words by heart and to repeat them at the proper time? This must have been done in many cases, and yet sometimes criminals were so densely ignorant and stupid, or it might be merely bewildered, that they failed; then the wretch paid the penalty of his life. "*Suspendatur,*" wrote the scribe against his name, and off he was hauled. The endless repetition of this word proved too much for official patience, and with brutal brevity the inscription finally appears, "Sus." or "S."

And now the Neck-verse was free to everyone were he or were he not in holy orders, and he claimed the privilege after conviction, but in the reign of Henry VII. (1487) an important change was made. A person who claimed clergy was to be branded on the crown of his thumb with an "M" if he were a murderer, with a "T" if he were guilty of any other felony; if he "prayed his clergy" a second time this was refused him, unless he were actually in orders. Of course the mark on the thumb was to record his previous escape from justice. It was with this "Tyburn T" (as it was called in Elizabethan slang) that Ben Jonson was branded. It is only within the last few years that careful Mr Cordy Jeaffreson has exhumed the true story from the Middlesex County Records. The poet quarrelled and fought a duel with Gabriel Spencer, an actor, and probably a former colleague. The affair came off at Shoreditch. Jonson, with his rapier, which the indictment (for a reason explained in the chapter on "Deodands") values at three shillings, briskly attacked his opponent, and almost immediately gave him a thrust in the side, whereof Spencer died then and there. Ben was forthwith seized and thrown into prison. Whilst waiting his trial he said that spies were set on him, but he was too much for them, and afterwards all the judges got from him was but "Ay" and "No." Why spies should have been necessary in so plain a case is far from clear. It is more significant that a devoted priest succeeded in converting him for the time to Roman Catholicism, and he afterwards confessed to Drummond of Hawthornden that he had come near the gallows. However, what he said, or did not say, is of little weight as compared with the evidence of contemporary judicial records. The fact is clear that the poet of *Every Man in his Humour*, the cunning artist of *Queen and Huntress*, and *Drink to me only with thine Eyes*, had a true bill found against him by the grand jury, who sat, by the way, in a tavern, for as yet Hicks Hall, the predecessor of the Session's-House on Clerkenwell Green, was not.

In October 1598, he was taken to the Old Bailey to stand his trial. He pleaded guilty, asked for the book, read like a clerk ("Jonson's learned sock," forsooth!), and as the strangely abbreviated Latin of the record has it, "*sign' cum lra' T et del*," that is, marked with the letter "T," and set at large to repair to "The Sun," "The Bolt," "The Triple Tun," or some other of those dim, enchanting Elizabethan taverns, there to give such an account of the transaction as sufficed to dissemble it till this age of grubbers and dictionaries wherein you are destined to nose every ancient scandal as you go up the staircase of letters. It has been suggested that the officer, moved to inexplicable tenderness, touched him with a cold iron. The only ground for this is that Dekker, in his savage Satiro Mastix; or, *The Untrussing of the Humourous Poet*, makes no reference to the "Tyburn T." One fancies that Ben speedily acquired a trick of carrying his hand so that the mark was not readily seen, or he may have cut or burnt it out as others did. All the same, the best evidence shows it to have been there.

In the reign of James I. another change was made. Women got the benefit of clergy in certain cases, and afterwards they were put on the same footing as men. Then in 1705 the necessity for reading was abolished, and in 1779 so was branding.

But another process was going on all this time. A great and ever-increasing number of crimes were declared to be without benefit of clergy. The selection was somewhat capricious. Among the exempted felonies were abduction with intent to marry, stealing clothes off the racks, stealing the kings' stores, and so on. Naturally the whole subject fell into inextricable confusion, and when it was abolished in 1827, even pedants must have given a sigh of relief. One detail escaped the reformer: since the time of Edward VI. every peer ("though he cannot read," saith the statute) enjoyed a privilege akin to that of clergy, and it was not till 1841 that this last vestige of the system vanished from the statute-book. I will only add that, in its details, "benefit of clergy" was even more grotesque and fantastic than it has here been possible to set forth.

PEINE FORTE ET DURE

In England during many centuries a prisoner was called to the bar before trial and enjoined to hold up his right hand, by which act he was held to admit himself the person named in the indictment. The clerk then asked him, "How say you, are you guilty or not guilty?" If he answered, "Not guilty," the next question was: "Culprit, how will you be tried?" to which he responded, "By God and my country." "God send you a good deliverance," rejoined the official, and the trial went forward. If the accused missed any of these responses, or would not speak at all, and if the offence were treason or a misdemeanour, his silence was taken for confession of guilt, and sentence was passed forthwith. If the charge were felony, a jury was empanelled to try whether he stood "mute of malice," or "mute by the visitation of God." If this last were found, the trial went on; if the other, he was solemnly warned by the judges of the terrible consequences summed up by Lord Coke (trial of Sir Richard Weston in 1615, for Sir Thomas Overbury's murder) in the three words—*onere, frigore, et fame*. The proceedings were most commonly adjourned to give him time for reflection; but if after every exhortation he remained obdurate, then he was adjudged to suffer the *peine forte et dure*. The judgment of the Court was in these words: "That you return from whence you came, to a low dungeon into which no light can enter; that you be stripped naked save a cloth about your loins, and laid down, your back upon the ground; that there be set upon your body a weight of iron as great as you can bear—and greater; that you have no sustenance, save on the first day three morsels of the coarsest bread, on the second day three draughts of stagnant water from the pool nearest the prison door, on the third day again three morsels of bread as before, and such bread and such water alternately from day to day; till you be pressed to death; your hands and feet tied to posts, and a sharp stone under your back."

There is but one rational way to discuss an institution of this sort. Let us trace out its history, for thus only can we explain how it came to have an existence at all. For the prisoner himself there was usually a very strong reason why *he* should stand mute. If he were convicted of felony his goods were forfeited; while in case of capital felony, the result of attainder was corruption of blood so that he could neither inherit nor transmit landed property. Often he must have known that conviction was certain. Had he fondness enough for his heirs—children or other—to make him choose this hideous torture instead of milder methods whereby the law despatched the ordinary convict from this world? Well, very many underwent the punishment. Between 1609-1618 the number was thirty-two (three of them women) in rural Middlesex alone. "*Mortuus en pen' fort' et dur'*," so the clerk wrote for epitaph against each name, and something still stranger than the penalty itself is revealed to us by an examination of the original records. Many of the culprits were evidently totally destitute, and these underwent the *peine forte et dure* from stupidity, obstinacy, or sheer indifference to mortal suffering and death.

The custom of pressing did not obtain its full development at once, and there is some difficulty as to how it began. A plausible explanation is given in Pike's "History of Crime," and is supported by the authority of the late Mr Justice Stephen. At one time a man charged with a serious offence was tried by ordeal; but by paying money to the king, it was possible to get the exceptional privilege of a trial by jury. Thus, when the accused was asked how he would be tried, his answer originally ran, "by God" (equal to by ordeal), or "by my country" (equal to by jury), since to put yourself on the country meant to submit yourself to this last. But trial by ordeal was abolished about 1215, and the alternative was a privilege to be claimed, not a necessity to be endured. Offenders soon discovered that by standing mute and declining to claim this privilege, they put the Court in a difficulty. The ideas of those distant days were simple exceedingly, and a legal form had strange force and efficacy. To put a prisoner before a jury without his consent was not to be thought of; but how to get his consent? At first the knot was rather cut than loosened. Thus, in some cases, the accused were put to death right off for not consenting to be tried "according to the law and custom of the realm." Then this was held too severe, and under Edward I., in the proceedings of the Parliament of Westminster, occurs the earliest definite mention of the punishment. It was enacted that notorious felons refusing to plead should be confined in the *prison forte et dure*. Here they went "barefooted and bareheaded, in their coat only in prison, upon the bare ground continually night and day, fastened down with irons," and only eating and drinking on alternate days as already set forth. It was bad enough, no doubt, but not of necessity fatal. So the authorities perceived, and they again cut the knot by a policy of starvation. So one infers from the case of Cecilia, wife of John Rygeway, in the time of Edward III. Cecilia was indicted for the murder of her husband; she refused to plead. Being committed to prison, she lived without meat or drink for forty days; and this being set down to the Virgin Mary, she was thereupon allowed to go free. This procedure seems to have been found too slow, and the increase of business at the assizes seemed like to end in a hopeless block. Were the judges to encamp in a country town while the prisoners made up their mind as to pleading? Something was wanted to "mend or end" the stubborn rascals; and under Henry IV., in the beginning of the fifteenth century, the "prison" *forte et dure* became the "peine" *forte et dure*: with the consequence that, if the accused declined to plead, there was an end of him in a few hours, the provision of bread and water being a mere remnant of the older form of sentence. This procedure lasted till 1772, when the 12 Geo. III., c. 20 made "standing mute in cases of felony equivalent to conviction." In 1827 it was enacted by 7 and 8 Geo. IV., c. 28, "that in such cases a plea of not guilty should be entered for the person accused." The curious formal dialogue between the clerk and the prisoner was abolished that same year. Something stronger than exhortation was now and again used before the obdurate prisoner was sentenced to pressing, thus at the Old Bailey in 1734, the thumbs of one John Durant were tied together with whipcord, which the executioner strung up hard and tight in presence of the Court; he was promised the *peine forte et dure* if this did not answer, but upon a little time being given him for reflection, he speedily made up his mind to plead not guilty.

It is difficult to explain the distinction drawn between ordinary felony on the one hand and treason and misdemeanours on the other. Perhaps the explanation is that the last, being much lighter offences, were never made the subject of trial by ordeal, and that treason being a crime endangering the very existence of the State, a sort of necessity compelled the judge to proceed in the most summary manner. No student of English History needs to be reminded that a trial for treason resulted almost as a matter of course in a conviction for treason. Peers of the realm had many privileges, but they were not exempt from the consequences of standing mute. Nor, as already noted, were women. Perhaps it were unreasonable to expect a criticism of the system from contemporary judges or text writers; but what they did say was odd enough; they did not condemn pressing, but they highly extolled the clemency of the law which directed the Court to reason with and admonish the accused before it submitted him to this dread penalty.

I shall now give some examples of practice. Fortunately (or unfortunately you may think as you read) we have at least one case recorded in great detail, though, curiously enough, it has escaped the notice of an authority so eminent as Mr Justice Stephen.

Margaret Clitherow was pressed to death at York on Lady Day, March 25th, 1586, and the story thereof was written by John Mush, secular priest, and her spiritual director. Margaret's husband was a Protestant, though his brother was a priest, and all his children appear to have been of the older faith. Accused of harbouring Jesuit and Seminary priests, of hearing mass, and so on, she was committed to York Castle, and in due time was arraigned in the Common Hall. In answer to the usual questions, she said that she would be tried "by God and by your own consciences," and refused to make any other answer. It was sheer obstinacy: she was a married woman, and she could have lost nothing by going to trial. But she coveted martyrdom, which everybody concerned appears, at first at any rate, to have been anxious to deny her. It was plainly intimated that if she would let herself be tried she would escape: "I think the country," said Clinch, the senior judge, "cannot find you guilty upon the slender evidence." The proceedings were adjourned, and the same night "Parson Whigington, a Puritan preacher," came and argued with her, apparently in the hope of persuading her to plead; but he failed to change her purpose; the next day she was brought back to the Hall. Something of a wrangle ensued between herself and Clinch, and in the end the latter seemed on the point of pronouncing sentence. Then Whigington stood up and began to speak; "the murmuring and noise in the Hall would not suffer him to be heard;" but he would not be put off, and "the judge commanded silence to hear him." He made a passionate appeal to the Court ("Did not perhaps God open the mouth of Balaam's ass?" is the somewhat ungracious comment of Father Mush.) "My lord," said he, "take heed what you do. You sit here to do justice; this woman's case is touching life and death, you ought not, either by God's law or man's, to judge her to die upon the slender witness of a boy;" with much more to the same effect. Clinch was at his wits' end, and went so far as to entreat the prisoner to plead in the proper form: "Good woman, I pray you put yourself to the country. There is no evidence but a boy against you, and whatsoever they (the jury) do, yet we may show mercy afterwards." She was moved not a whit; and then Rhodes, the other judge, broke in: "Why stand we all day about this naughty, wilful woman?" Yet once again she was entreated, but as vainly as before; it was evident that the law must take its course; and "then the judge bade the sheriff look to her, who pinioned her arms with a cord." She was carried back to prison through the crowd, of whom some said, "She received comfort from the Holy Ghost;" others, "that she was possessed of a merry devil." When her husband was told of her condemnation, "he fared like a man out of his wits, and wept so vehemently that the blood gushed out of his nose in great quantity." Some of the Council suggested that she was with child. There seems to have been some foundation for the remark, at any rate, Clinch caught eagerly at the idea. "God defend she should die if she be with child," said he several times, when the sheriff asked for directions, and others of sterner mould were pressing for her despatch. Kind-hearted Whigington tried again and again to persuade her; and the Lord Mayor of York, who had married her mother ("a rich widow which died before this tragedy the summer last"), begged her on his knees, "with great show of sorrow and affection," to pronounce the words that had such strange efficacy. It was all in vain, so at last even Whigington abandoned his attempt, and "after he had pitied her case awhile, he departed and came no more."

Her execution was fixed for Friday, and the fact was notified to her the night before. In the early morning of her last day on earth she quietly talked the matter over with another woman. "I will procure," the woman said, "some friends to lay weight on you, that you may be quickly despatched from your pain." She answered her that it must not be. At eight the sheriffs came for her, and "she went barefoot and barelegged, her gown loose about her." The short street was crowded with people to whom she dealt forth alms. At the appointed place, one of the sheriffs, "abhorring the cruel fact, stood weeping at the door;" but the other, whose name was Fawcett, was of harder stuff. He "commanded her to put off her apparel," whereupon she and the other woman "requested him, on their knees, that she might die in her smock, and that for the honour of womankind they would not see her naked." That could not be granted, but they were allowed to clothe her in a long habit of linen she had herself prepared for the occasion. She now lay down on the ground. On her face was a handkerchief. A door was laid upon her. "Her hands she joined towards her face"; but Fawcett said they must be bound, and bound they were to two posts, "so that her body and her arms made a perfect cross." They continued to vex the passing soul with vain words, but at last they put the weights on the door. In her intolerable anguish she gave but a single cry: "Jesu! Jesu! Jesu! have mercy upon me!" Then there was stillness; though the end was not yet. "She was in dying one quarter of an hour. A sharp stone as much as a man's fist put under her back, upon her was laid a quantity of seven or eight hundredweight to the least, which, breaking her ribs, caused them, to burst forth of the skin." It was now nine in the morning, but not till three of the afternoon were the braised remains taken from the press.

Stories of violence and cruelty serve not our purpose unless they illustrate some point, and I shall but refer to two other cases.

Major Strangeways was arraigned in 1658 (under the Commonwealth be it noted) for the murder of his brother-in-law. In presence of the coroner's jury he was made to take the corpse by the hand and touch its wounds, for it was supposed that, if he were guilty, these would bleed afresh. There was no bleeding, but this availed him nothing, and he was put on his trial at the Old Bailey in due course. He refused to plead, and made no secret of his motive; he foresaw conviction, and desired to prevent the forfeiture of his estate. He was ordered to undergo the *peine forte et dure*. The press was put on him angle-wise; it was enough to hurt, but not to kill, so the bystanders benevolently added their weight, and in ten minutes all was over. The dead body was then displayed to the public.

Again, in 1726, a man named Burnworth was arraigned at Kingston for murder. At first he refused to plead, but after being pressed for an hour and three-quarters with four hundredweight of iron, he yielded. He was carried back to the dock, said he was not guilty, and was tried, convicted, and hanged. There was at least one case in the reign of George II.—but enough of such horrors.

A PASSAGE IN SHAKESPEARE

FINES AND RECOVERIES

"Is this the fine of his fines, and the recovery of his recoveries, to have his fine pate full of fine dust? Will his vouchers vouch him no more of his purchases, and double ones too, than the length and breadth of a pair of indentures?" Thus the Prince of Denmark moralising in the graveyard scene in Hamlet over the skull of a supposed lawyer: with more to the same effect, all showing that Shakespeare had a knowledge of law terms remarkable in a layman, and that he used them with curious precision. In the huge body of Shakespearian literature there are special works (one by Lord Chancellor Campbell) on the fact, which has been used to buttress up the Baconian authorship theory (indeed, it is the only positive fact at all in point). Again, it has been conjectured that the dramatist spent some time in a lawyer's office, and that phrases from the deeds he engrossed stuck in his memory. It is far more likely that, being the man of his age he was, he would read in and round the law as well as much else for its own sake, and that fines and recoveries were so odd in themselves, and so excellently illustrative of English history and procedure, that they fairly took his mighty fancy.

Recoveries were already some two hundred years old in his time, and, to judge from the tone of the passage, people must even then have held them in derision. But they were to last full two hundred years more; for not till 1833 did they vanish from the scene. Recoveries were methods of disentailing an estate by means of a complicated series of fictions. They arose in this way:—Before 1285, when land was given to a man and the heirs of his body, the judges ruled that, the moment a son was born, the father held the estate as a simple freehold, which he could sell or make away with very much as he chose. The great landowners were ill-content at this; they meant their tenants to enjoy their estates only as long as they rendered useful service in return, and if issue failed a man, they thought the land should revert to his lord on his death. Hence in that year an act procured by their influence, called *De Donis Conditionalibus*, or the Statute of Westminster the Second (13 Ed. I., c. 1), created the Estate Tail (*i.e. Taillé*, or restricted). It provided that land given to a man and his heirs as above, reverted to the original donor on failure of the donee's issue. Blackstone waxes eloquent over the evils that ensued. Children declined obedience to a father who could not disinherit; farmers lost their leases, which had no force against the heir; and creditors were defrauded of their debts, which constituted no charge on the land, nay, treasons were fostered, insomuch as the traitor's interest lapsing at his death, nothing was left for the king to seize. Yet it was not till the reign of Edward IV. that a device was found to evade the Statute. *Taltarum's Case* was decided in 1472. It is loosely said that this established the validity of recoveries, but they were in use some time before, and Sir Frederick Pollock will have it that it was the oddity of the name which made a landmark of the decision. A Recovery was a sort of friendly or fictitious action, whereby the estate was adjudged to an outsider, whose claim, though baseless—if one did not look beyond the four corners of the action—was acquiesced in by the nominal defendant.

The mediæval lawyer was usually a priest, and he had found those entails grievous obstacles in the way of the Church's aggrandisement. Perhaps, too, as the country grew in wealth, so rigid a law of settlement bore hard on an ever-waxing commercial class. To repeal the Statute seemed impossible, but the great landowners, while proof against force and impermeable to argument, were not hard to outwit. A legal complication passed their understanding; and this one, however brazen, had the patronage of many powerful interests. Thus, and thus only, may the fact of their acquiescence be explained.

And now let us trace out the steps in a common recovery with "double voucher." The judges had already made one preparatory breach in the law. A tenant in tail could dispose of his estate if he left other lands of the same value; for these his heirs held under the same conditions as the original property. The principle of this decision was ingeniously used as a lever to overthrow the system.

Suppose A, tenant in tail, had contracted to sell his land to B: he began by formally disposing of it to C, usually his attorney, and technically called "Tenant to the *præcipe*," or writ. Then B commenced an action in the Common Pleas against C to recover the estate in question, which, he asserted, had been wrongfully taken from him. C, instead of defending the action, "vouched to warranty" A: that is, he called in A to defend, on the ground that the said A had covenanted to support his title; but A, instead of defending the action, "vouched to warranty" D. This last, called the "common vouchee" (in the form in Blackstone he appears as "Jacob Morland"), was always the "Crier to the Court," and for playing his part received the modest fee of fourpence on each recovery. At first he (Jacob) made a great show at fight; he denied all B's statements, and "put himself upon the country:" *i.e.* he demanded that the case should go before a jury for trial. B then craved leave "to imparl" (*i.e.* to have a private conference with Jacob), and the proceedings were solemnly adjourned. When they were resumed Jacob was not to be found: "he hath (it was adjudged) departed in contempt of the Court." Evidently, or so it seemed, he had no answer to make. Then B's claim was allowed; C was to have of the lands of A a quantity equal to what he had nominally lost; whilst A, in his turn, was to have the same remedy against Jacob, who, having no means at all, cheerfully accepted much paper responsibility. Then a writ was issued to the sheriff of the county wherein the lands were situate, directing him to give possession to B, whose title was constituted by a record of all the aforesaid transactions.

As the centuries went by the proceedings became ever less substantial, the action was always commenced by the issue of a writ in the usual way, but most of the other steps were only taken on paper. Sir Frederick Pollock says, that if the disentailer were a peer, a sergeant was actually briefed to move the court in the matter: also, one must note that lands held from the crown were never subject to this process (nor can they now be disentailed without a special act of Parliament). By another barefaced fiction, colonial property might be disentailed in England. The deed roundly asserted that the island of Antigua (or wherenot) lay in the parish of St Mary, Islington—the operation of this geographical miracle giving jurisdiction to the Court of Common Pleas. One would suppose that something simpler might have served; but though laymen jeered, lawyers regarded these quaint formalities with strange reverence. My Lord Coke mentions with solemn reprobation a counsel named Hoord who scoffed thereat in the House of Lords, and whom a judge gravely rebuked as not worthy to be of the profession of the law, for that he "durst speak against common recoveries;" and as late as 1820, Thomas Coventry, Esq., of Lincoln's Inn, concludes his learned treatise on the subject with an eloquent if slightly confused protest against any change, "which could know no end but an apparent confusion, or clearing away a path for the access of some modern Pretender to strip the ivy from the venerable oak of our boasted constitution, the only emblem that remains of its antiquity and endurance."

And now for a word on fines. These were so called for that they made an end of a controversy. They were simpler and even more ancient than recoveries. A fictitious action was begun by the purchaser against the vendor of an estate, wherein the latter soon gave in: the case was compromised, a fine was paid to the Crown, upon the Court giving its consent to this termination of the proceedings, and the record thereof became the purchaser's title. They were likewise used to bar entails, though they were not so effectual as recoveries. One of the first Acts of the Reform Parliament of 1833 was the Statute for the Abolition of Fines and Recoveries. It was a mere question of procedure, for the law itself remained unaltered: but disentailment was effected by the enrolment of a deed in Chancery. And now the dust lies thick on shelves of text-books—a whole system of learning, full of intricate details, the creation of centuries of perverse ingenuity.

And the land-owners? These, too, long since availed themselves of the dark and subtle devices of the conveyancer. Sir Orlando Bridgman, a great lawyer of the Commonwealth, and finally Chief Justice of the Common Pleas under Charles II., invented and perfected the system of family settlements which to-day secures the secular interests of our great historic houses, as well as, if less directly than, any enactment could do.

THE CUSTOM OF THE MANOR

Has chance or necessity ever opened to you the charter-chest of the respectable solicitor in some country town? Then, among his records, you have noted an interminable series of parchment volumes—very thick, very closely written, some centuries old, and one in current use. These are the court-rolls of the Manor of Wherenot. If you can spell out the beautifully written mediæval characters, you are sure to light on many a quaint record of by-gone folk and their ways, for, better than aught else, the manor and its muniments preserve for us the English past.

Manors, they used to say, arose in this fashion. A great lord obtained a piece of land from the King; part he disposed of to tenants who held of him in freehold (this sub-infeudation was stopped by the statute *quia emptores* in 1290); the rest was his domain, on part of which he built the manor house, another part was cultivated by villeins, then the cotters had dwellings with portions of land, and the residue was waste, where the folk of the manor pastured their cattle, gathered fuel, and made their ways. Sometimes these villeins were slaves, but each had his patch of soil, wherefor he rendered some servile office to his lord, ploughing his land, garnering his crops, or such like. The business of the manor was transacted in two courts, the Court Baron and the Customary Court. The first was attended by the freeholders, who themselves constituted the Court; the second by the villeins, who merely hearkened to and witnessed the doings of the lord or his steward. When a villein died, the fact that the new tenant had such and such a field on condition of rendering so many days' labour yearly was noted in the records or roll of the Customary Court, and this roll, or a copy of it, becoming his title, he was dubbed a copyholder. In theory he was a mere tenant at the will of the lord, but time fettered the lord's will, until the principle was evolved that it must be exercised according to the custom of the manor, for "custom" as Lord Coke put it, "is the life of the manor," and so it came about that the holder had fixity of tenure while he did his service. His position steadily improved, the slave became free, the servile toil a money payment, and now the court agenda merely register changes of title. This account of the manor may serve for description, but does not represent the real origin, which has not yet been exactly ascertained. It was a fragment of Old England, with a lord usually of Norman race as head, and the relations between head and members elaborated and controlled by the theories and devices of the mediæval lawyer. As manorial law was custom, old local usages were preserved unaltered; thus, whilst the root idea of feudalism was that the eldest son should inherit his father's land, and the manor itself did so descend, within it an extraordinary diversity of usage obtained. By a custom similar to that of Gavelkind (in Kent), the copyholder's estate was sometimes parted equally among all his sons. In other places, Borough-English prevailed, that is, the youngest son took everything, to the exclusion of his elder brothers; nay, by an odd application of the maxim "better late than never," a posthumous child ousted the brother already in possession; or, again, the widow or widower inherited. When the tenant died, the lord had a right to seize his best chattel (usually a beast), this was called a Heriot, and it is yet here and there exacted. Many customs are old Saxon, many customs were invented, or at any rate twisted into fantastic rights from mere whim or a not very cleanly sense of humour, but here one must often merely accept the fact, for to try it by the rule of right reason were absurd.

Most manors were held of the Crown, in return for services sometimes of the oddest character; thus, Solomon De Campis (or Solomon At-Field) had land in Kent on condition that, "as often as our lord the King would cross the sea, the said Solomon and his heirs should go along with him to hold his head on the sea, if it was needful;" and certain jurors solemnly present on their oath that "the aforesaid Solomon fully performed the aforesaid service." Our early kings provided against every possible contingency. One tenant enjoyed land by the service of holding the King's stirrup when he mounted his horse at Cambridge Castle. Another must make *hastias* in the King's kitchen on the day of his coronation. The glossaries are dumb as to this mysterious dish, though the learned darkly hint at haggis! Or was it "a certain potage called the mess of *Giron*," which, being enriched with lard, was called *Maupygernon*—which last is possibly mediæval Welsh for a haggis? Thomas Bardolf, who died, lord of Addington, in 5 Edward III., was pledged to compound three portions of this dainty dish against Coronation Day, and serve them up smoking hot, one to the King, one to his Grace of Canterbury, and the third "to whomsoever the King would." Other manors were held on the tenure of presenting to the King a white young brach ("lady the brach" of *King Lear*) with red ears; of delivering a hundred herrings baked in twenty pasties; of finding the King a penny for an oblation, whenever he came to hear mass at Maplescamp, in Kent: gifts of roses, falcons, capons (which last dainties your mediæval sovereign held in special favour), were abundant. But how to riddle this one? The manor of Shrivenham, in Berks, was held (*temp.* Edward III.) by the family of Becket, whose head, whenever the King passed over a certain bridge in those parts, must present himself with two white capons, whereto he directed the royal attention in choice mediæval Latin, "Behold," he said, "my lord, these two capons, which you shall have another time, but not now," which pleasantry reminds one of the current vulgarism, "Will you have it now, or wait till you get it?" The service of the Dymocks, owners of Scrivelsby in Lincoln, as King's champions, and of the Duke of Norfolk, as Earl Marshal of England, curious enough in themselves, are too notorious for this crowded page.

A few quaint tenures are of quite modern origin. Thus the honour of Woodstock (an honour was a lordship over several manors: so "Waverley Honour" in Scott's great romance) is held by the tenure of presenting a banner each second of August at Windsor Castle; that being the anniversary of Blenheim, fought in 1704; and on each 18th of June the Duke of Wellington must likewise send to the same place, for the estate of Strathfieldsay, a tri-coloured flag to commemorate Waterloo. The last century legal antiquary pricked up his ears at a fine scandal which he fondly imagined in connection with the manors of Poyle and Catteshill, both near Guildford. Their holders were bound to provide a certain number (twelve in one instance) of young women, called *meretrices,* for the service of the royal court. Dry-as-dust shook his solemn head, invented pimp-tenure (a "peculiarly odious kind of tenure" he explained), and the forerunner of the man who writes to *The Times* (it was then to the *Gentleman's Magazine*) cracked some not particularly choice jokes on the subject. A wider knowledge restored the moral character of the King, his lords, and the much-slandered young women, whose decent dust may now repose in peace. In mediæval Latin the word was widely used for the female servant general or special, and these were, it seems, neither more nor less than laundry-maids.

Manors of an early date were ofttimes held under other manors on equally whimsical conditions. A snowball at summer and a red rose at Christmas are extravagantly picturesque. A hawk was a common rent; but in one case it was carried to the Earl of Huntingdon's house, by the yielder, attended by his wife, three boys, three horses, and three greyhounds; and these must be housed for forty days at the earl's expense, while his countess must give the lady her second best gown. Again, the tenant of Brindwood in Essex, upon every change, must come with his wife, his man, and his maid, all a-horseback to the rectory, "with his hawke on his fist and his greyhound in his slip"; he blows three blasts with his horn, and then receives curious gifts, and thereafter departeth. The lord of the Manor of Essington, in Stafford, must bring a goose every New Year's Day to the head manor-house at Hilton. Here he drives it about the fire, which Jack of Hilton blows furiously, and (one regrets to add) most improperly. But Jack may be forgiven, for he is but "an image of brass about twelve inches high," whose description you read at length in old Thomas Blount, the great recorder of all these mad pranks.

The holding of Pusey in Berks by the Pusey Horn, gifted, it is said, by King Canute, is well-known. Sir Philip de Somerville, knight, was bound to hunt and capture the Earl of Lancaster's *greese* (wild swine) for my lord's larder upon St Peter's Day in August. This he did till Holy-Rood Day, when he dined with the steward, and after dinner "he shall kiss the porter and depart." This same Sir Philip de Somerville held the Manor of Whychenover at half terms from the Earl on condition that there ever hung in his hall one bacon flitch to be assigned to a happy married couple yearly in Lent, after a variety of ceremonies like those in the more famous case of Dunmow: the disposal of the flitch there being likewise according to "the custom of the manor."

In the customs that made up the inner life of the manor one finds a diversity too great for classification. However, those old English folk were a merry lot; with usages not sad nor savage, but having much sensible joy in good meat and drink. At Baldock, in Hertfordshire, the Customary Court was holden at dinner-time, whereto every baker and vintner within the bounds must send bread and ale which the steward and his jury "cam' to pree," and presently gave their verdict "if these be wholesome for man's body or no." To the Manor of Hutton Conyers there was attached a great common, where many townships pastured their sheep; and the shepherd of each township "did fealty by bringing to the Court a large apple pie, and a twopenny sweet cake." For refreshment, "furmity and mustard, well mixed in an earthen pot, is placed before the shepherds, which they sup with spoons provided by themselves, and if any forget his spoon then, for so the customary law wills it, he must lay him down upon his belly, and sup the furmity with his face to the pot or dish." And the custom further permits the bystanders "to dip his face into the furmity," to the great delight of all present. To finer issues is the money provided by Magdalen College, Oxford, for certain manors of theirs in Hampshire, *pro mulieribus hockantibus*, as the dog Latin of the college accounts hath it. On Hock Day, annually, "the women stop the ways with ropes, and pull passengers to them, desiring something to be laid out in pious uses": the men having hocked the women after the same fashion the day before. There are traces of this usage further afield than Hampshire. Not less jovial were the tenants of South Malling, in Kent, who were bound to pay scot-ale, which fund they agreeably expended in "drink with the bedel of the Lord Archbishop." The case of Stamford, in Lincoln, is noteworthy as showing the origin of one peculiar custom. In the time of King John, William, Earl Warren, was lord of the place. One day he saw from his castle wall "two bulls fighting for a cow in the castle meadow;" their bellowing attracted all the butcher's dogs in the place; and these, in company with a host of rag-tag and bobtail, chased one of the champions in and out the town till he went mad; all which so delighted Earl Warren, that he forthwith gifted the common to the butchers on condition that they provided a mad bull six weeks before Christmas Day, "for the continuance of that sport for ever."

It is impossible even to conjecture the origin of other customs. In most manors, when a copy-holder died, his widow had in free-bench (or what the common law calls dower) the whole or part of his lands. There was one restriction: she must remain "sole and chaste." Yet, if she forgot herself, her case was not altogether past praying for in the Manor of Enborne in Berkshire. At the next Customary Court she appeared strangely mounted upon a black ram, her face to the tail, the which grasping in her hand, she recited, sure the merriest, maddest rhyme it ever entered into the heart of man to conceive—

"Here I am
Riding upon a black ram"——

Alas, that the rest must be silence! The *Spectator*, greatly daring, gives it in full; but that was as far back as November 1st, 1714. A like custom ruled the Manor of Kilmersdon, in Somerset, where the doggerel, if briefer and blunter, is at least equally gross. And here one must refer to the *jus primæ noctis*, that lewd historic jest which, in England at any rate, was ever a sheer delusion. True that on the marriage of a villein's daughter a fine was paid to the lord, but this was not to spare her blushes, but as compensation to him for the loss of her services—inasmuch as she took the domicile of her husband. Nay, the custom of the manor usually made for morality. There was a fine called child-wit exacted on the birth of an illegitimate child, sometimes from the infant's father, or, again, from the father of its mother. Nay, in one or two places the unlucky lover forfeited all his goods and chattels. On the other hand a curious privilege attached to an oak in Knoll Wood in the Manor of Terley in Staffordshire: "In case oath were made that the bastard was got within the umbrage or reach of its boughs," neither spiritual nor temporal power had ought to say, and the man got off scot free.

The curious tenacity of the manorial custom is well shown in the case of Pomber in Hampshire: the Annual Court, in accordance with immemorial usage, must be held in the open air, but the inconvenience of this was obviated by an immediate adjournment of the proceedings to the nearest tavern. The records were not kept on parchment, but "on a piece of wood called a tally, about three feet long and an inch and a half square, furnished every day by the steward." In time these strange muniments became worm-eaten and illegible; and, as occupying much needed room, were thrown to the flames by the dozen. (It will be remembered that the old Houses of Parliament were set on fire and destroyed on the burning of the exchequer tallies, October 1834.) Some of the survivors were produced as evidence in a case heard at Winchester, which fact provoked "a counsellor on the opposite side of the question" to dub it "a wooden cause." The obvious retort—that his was a wooden joke—seems lacking; but possibly this gem of legal humour emanated from the Bench: how often one has seen its like!

Still stranger was the Lawless Court of the Honour of Raleigh: it was held in the darkness of cockcrow; the steward and the suitors (i.e., those bound to attend the Court) mumbled their words in scarce audible fashion; candles, pens, ink, were all forbidden; for, as the authorities vaguely put it, "they supply that office with a coal." To ensure a punctual attendance, the suitor "forfeits to his lord double his rent every hour he is absent." The learned Camden affirms it was all to punish the aboriginal tenants for a conspiracy hatched in the darkness of the night; again he sees in it a remnant of an old Teutonic custom; and in the end you suspect that he knows as little as yourself.

Then there was the white bull which the tenants of the monks of Bury St Edmunds were bound by their leases to provide, that childless women might present it to the shrine of the martyred king of East Anglia; there was the fine called "thistletake," which the owner of beasts crossing the common, and snatching at the "symbol dear," must pay to the lord of the Manor of Halton; there are the "three clove-gillieflowers" which the tenants of Hame in Surrey shall render at the King's coronation; there are all sorts of minute details as to house-bote and fire-bote, and common of piscary and turbary. One more custom and we have done. In the time of Richard the Lion-heart, Randal Blundeville, Earl of Chester, was on one occasion sore pressed by the Flintshire Welsh. He summoned to his aid his constable of Cheshire, one Roger Lacy, "for his fierceness surnamed Hell." It was fair-time at Chester, and Roger, putting himself at the head of the motley crowd marched off to his relief. The Welsh heard, saw, and bolted, and the grateful earl there and then promulgated a charter granting to Roger and his heirs for ever, "power over all fiddlers, lechers, light ladies (the charter has a briefer and stronger term), and cobblers in Chester." Under Henry VII. we find the then grantee exacting from the minstrels (*inter alia*) "four flagons of wine and a lance," whilst each of the aforesaid ladies must pay fourpence on the feast of St John the Baptist. Under Elizabeth, various acts were aimed at rogues, vagabonds, and sturdy beggars, but always with a saving provision as to this Chester jurisdiction, and in later times the Vagrant Act (17 George II., cap. 5) had a like reservation.

DEODANDS

At one time or other you have looked, one supposes, into that huge collection of curiosities and horrors known as the State Trials. You may possibly have noted the form of indictment in the murder cases; and if so, one odd detail must have impressed you. Having set forth the weapon used by the murderer, the document invariably goes on to estimate its money value: for, having been instrumental in taking human life, it was forfeit to the Crown, and it or its price had to be duly accounted for. It was called a Deodand, but the name was applied to many things besides arms used with malice aforethought. Thus, a man died by misadventure: then was the material cause active or passive? For instance, his end might come because a tree fell on him, or because he fell from a tree, in either case the wood was a deodand, and so forfeited. The name is from *Deo dandum*—a thing that must be offered to God, and this because in early mediæval times the Church or the poor had the ultimate benefit.

For the origin of the custom one must go far back. In Hebrew, Greek, and Roman legislation, the physical object that caused the loss of human life was held accursed, and hence was destroyed or forfeited. In England a thing became a deodand only when the coroner's jury (or more rarely some other authority) had found it the cause of death; which death, moreover, must happen within a year and a day of the accident. If it did, the thing was seized, no matter where it was, or who had it. In default of delivery the township was liable, and it was the Sheriff's duty to get the value therefrom. If a man had *per infortunium* (or without blame) used the article, the jury found that as a fact, and he was acquitted, or rather pardoned; but in strict law his goods were forfeit as late as 1828. And not everything causing death was a deodand. If a man fell into the water, was carried under a mill-wheel, and perished, the wheel was forfeit but not the mill. The distinction was sometimes difficult. Here are two actual examples. A cart and a waggon came into collision; the man in the cart was pitched out under the waggon-wheels and died. The two vehicles, all they held, the horses that drew them, were adjudged deodands, "because they all moved *ad mortem*." Again, a ship was hauled up for repairs, toppled over on a shipwright at work, and was declared forfeit. Your mediæval lawyer was nothing if not subtle, and he soon raised doubts enough to gravel a schoolman. He questioned if things fixed to the freehold could become deodands. Suppose a man were ringing a church bell, and the rope, getting twisted round his windpipe in some strange fashion, choked the life out of him: how then? The rope seemed past praying for, but what about the bell? The learned differed, yet all agreed that if the timber holding the bell got loose, and came crashing down on the sexton, the royal treasury, of clear right, pounced on rope, and bell, and timber. How furiously, with what a wealth of legal learning and invention, one fancies the utter barristers must have "mooted" those fascinating points after supper in the halls of their ancient Inns!

The decisions were hard to reconcile. Thus, in Edward the Third's time, it was held that if a man fall to his death from his horse against the trunk of a tree, the horse is forfeit, but not the tree. But in the same reign a distinction was drawn. One William Daventry, a servant to John Blaburgh, engaged in watering a horse, was grievously hurt. He was carried to his master's house *"apud Fleet Street in suburbio London"*, and there at even he died. At first the horse was adjudged a deodand, but Blaburgh got the inquisition quashed on the ground that the horse had not thrown his rider. Again, if a lad under fourteen fell from a cart and was killed, there was no deodand: as some opined, because the masses might be dispensed with, in the case of one presumed sinless from his tender age, and the proper end of deodands was to procure masses; but others urged it was "because he was not of discretion to look to himself." The further question—what possible difference this could make—was not raised; for even a mediæval lawyer's speculation must stop somewhere. But how if the slayer were a lad? A Cornish case, *temp.* 1302, supplies an answer. Jack of Burton, a boy of twelve, had a mind to draw the bow. He rigged up a target in a house, and shot thereat from the outside. One arrow missed the mark, and, glancing off a hook, transfixed a woman called Rose. Rose died forthwith, and Jack fled in horror. It was held that *le Hoke* was a deodand, but that the boy, on account of his age, was no whit to blame, and (with a touch of kindliness) a proclamation was made far and wide that he might return in safety. In this connection one recalls the awkward misadventure of Abbot, Archbishop of Canterbury, in the reign of James I., who, being out a-hunting, killed, by pure accident, Peter Hawkins, his keeper. He had many enemies, and all sorts of ecclesiastical and temporal penalties were threatened: at least, it was said, let all his goods be confiscate. But the King turned a deaf ear to these suggestions: he comforted the unlucky prelate with kindly words, and a full pardon, dated 26th September 1621, removed all possible danger from his reverend person.

If a man met his death afloat, there was deodand or no deodand as the water was fresh or salt, for these rules had no force on the high seas or in tidal rivers: because, said some, "there were so many deaths at sea." "Nay," said others, "how forfeit the ocean?" "But at least," it was replied, "one could take the ship"——but here again speculation must stop. Although deodands first went to the Crown, and were properly applied to pious or charitable uses, yet they were often granted to lords of manors: so often, indeed, that one of the few references to them in English literature—a couplet in Samuel Butler's *Hudibras*—treats this as the general rule.

> "For love should, like a deodand,
> Still fall to the owner of the land."

This owner was not seldom exacting, and his claim was met in characteristic English fashion. The coroner's jury returned the value of the deodand at next to nothing, *e.g.*, "a horse, value three shillings," and the Court of "King's Bench" refused to disturb the finding. Hence one absurdity balanced another, and the doctrine was long defended. In 1820, Joseph Chitty, in his standard work on *Prerogatives*, maintains that "the forfeiture is rational so far as it strengthens the natural sensation of the mind at the sudden destruction of human life." But in later years these mediæval ghosts began to walk again to some purpose. In 1840 the London and Birmingham Railway Company was amerced in £2000 as a deodand! Railway directors were no doubt convinced that 9 and 10 Vic., c. 62, which in 1846 made an end of the whole business, came not a day too soon. Had the law of twenty years before that been restored, there might have been some warrant for stripping those same directors of all their property after each railway accident, and one shudders to think of the consequences had the coroner's jury found the plant used not *per infortunium*.

One thing must be added, many held that the instruments of a murder, though forfeited to the Crown, were not, properly speaking, deodands, and they quoted as illustration the curious case of one Rempston, who forced his boat's crew to row under London Bridge *invitis corum dentibus* in dangerous weather. He was thrown out and drowned, and the jury, it was said, brought in a verdict of *felo de se*, to save the boat from forfeiture. But the weight of authority was emphatically against this view.

THE LAW OF THE FOREST

"A stretch of land, thick planted with trees;" so you picture a forest to yourself, but old English law held otherwise. There were miles of woodland that were not forest at all, and acres of pasture that were. John Manwood, the Elizabethan lawyer, still our chief authority on the subject, defines it as "a certain territory of woody grounds and fruitful pastures, privileged for wild beasts and fowls of forest, chase, and warren, to rest and abide in under the safe protection of the king." Such a preserve was exactly delimited, and might contain villages, churches, and so forth, within its bounds, as the New Forest does to-day. The king had certain rights over all, yet it was mainly private property; nay, there might be spaces in it, but not of it,—within its Bounds, but not within its Regard, as the phrase ran,—and so exempt from its peculiar laws. Manwood gives a picturesque, though quite erroneous derivation of the term: it was *For Rest* of the wild beasts; but a sounder etymology traces the word to *foris* (= outside), for that it was outside the jurisdiction of the Common Law, and had codes, courts, and officers of its own. The whole business was for centuries alike insult and wrong to the Commons of England.

Hunting was not merely the chief amusement of our early kings: it was a necessary pursuit for the keeping down of the wild beasts then a real danger to the fields and their cultivators. The Forest Charter of Canute the Dane (dated 1016) is a myth; but it is certain that, before the Conquest, the sovereign had a peculiar—howbeit, an undefined—property in the woodland. The Conqueror, who, according to the Saxon Chronicle, loved the tall deer as if he had been their father, devastated far and wide to make the New Forest; and he and his immediate successors punished hurt done to the deer with loss of life or limb. The Great Charter contained provisions against this odious abuse of power, and under Henry III. a special charter of the forest enacted that no man should lose life or limb for killing deer, at the same time that it disafforested (*i.e.*, removed from the forest to which they had been improperly joined) vast tracts of country. After the New there was but one other forest made in England, that was the land round Hampton Court, afforested under Henry VIII. by Act of Parliament.

An attempt to revive royal rights over the woodland hastened the fall of Charles the First, and then the Commonwealth gave the forest system its death-blow, though it was not till the time of George III. that the great mass of enactments was formally repealed. A Court of Swainmote lingers in the New Forest and elsewhere, and its officials, called Verderers, albeit shorn of their ancient power and splendour, do their quaint antics still; but by an odd, though happily not singular inversion, those old popular wrongs are now become popular privileges; Epping Forest, for instance, could never have become a public park but for the Crown rights, and these same rights over the woodlands throughout the country now yield an income which more than covers the cost of the whole Civil List. Had the Crown looked more sharply to its own, the profit to ourselves had been still vaster.

The forest laws, however complex in detail, were all inspired by one consistent idea—the preservation, to wit, of the king's venison. Even under Edward I.'s comparatively humane rule the verderer held an inquest upon a deer found dead in the Regard, just as the coroner did upon a man's body, and the jury found how the creature came to its end. The very arrows gleaned there were entered in the verderer's role. The freeholder within that charmed ground might not fell his own timber without leave, lest he should spoil the *Cover*: nor could he turn out his goats to browse, for they would taint the pasture; whilst he must feed his sheep in moderation, else he committed the grievous offence of *surcharging* the forest.

The forest had a huge staff of officers. First was a multitude of subordinates; foresters—who, if they kept ale-houses in the Regard, and encouraged folk to drink therein, committed a special crime called *Scotale*—agistors, woodwards, keepers, verminers, sub-verminers, and what not. These haled trespassers before the Court of Attachments, which was held every forty days. In command of them were the verderers, constituting, with representatives from the forest townships, the Court of Swainmote, which met thrice a year for (*inter alia*) the trial of the more important offences. Judgment on its findings was given at the Court of Justice Seat, held but once in the three years, under the presidency of a Lord Chief Justice in Eyre of the Forest. There were but two—one for the north, the other for the south of the Trent; and inasmuch as this officer was commonly some great noble—"A man," says my Lord Coke, with a touch of irony, "of greater dignity than of knowledge of the laws of the forest"—some skilled professional folk were joined with him in the commission. The last Court of Justice Seat was held in 1670 by the Earl of Oxford. It was a mere form: the last but one (in 1635) had created a fine pother by its exactions.

Offences were either trespasses *in Vert* or trespasses *in Venison*. The Vert (= green) was of course the cover; and the destruction thereof was called *Waste*, while *Assart* was stubbling it up to make ploughland: and *Purpestre* (a most grievous business) was building on or enclosing part of the forest. (As late as the reign of Charles I., Sir Sampson Darnell was heavily fined for erecting a windmill on his own ground in Windsor Chase). Moreover, Vert might be *Over Vert* or *Hault-Bois*, or it might be *Nether-Vert* or *Sous-Bois*, according as it was underwood or not; and in either case it was *Special Vert* if it bore fruit, such as pears, crabs, hips, and haws, whereon the deer might feed.

Venison, as lawyers understood it, was composed of Beasts of Forest—to wit, the hart, the hind, the hare, the boar, and the wolf—and Beasts of Chase. A Chase, which was like a park, but was not enclosed, might be held by a subject; but every forest was likewise a chase and a warren, and the beasts of chase were the buck, the doe, the martern, and the roe. These were described with wondrous detail. The hart—"the most stately beast which goeth on the earth, having as it were a majesty both in its gait and countenance"—was in his first year a Calf, in his second a Broket, in his third a Spayad, in his fourth a Staggard, in his fifth a Stag, and in his sixth a Hart. If he escaped the pursuit of king or queen he became a Hart Royal, which no subject might molest.

In 1194, Richard Cœur-de-Lion hunted a noble beast out of the forest of Sherwood into Barnsdale in Yorkshire, and there losing him, made proclamation "that no person should kill, hunt, or chase the said hart, but that he might safely return into the forest again." An animal thus honoured was called a Hart Royal Proclaimed, and in the 21st of King Henry VII., a man was indicted for taking so precious a life, but the case apparently went off for want of technical proof of proclamation. Your precise woodman talked of a Bevy of roes, a Richesse of marterns, a Lease of bucks. He said that a hart harboureth, whilst a buck lodgeth, and a hare was seated. He dislodged the buck, but he started the hare. He would tell you that the hart belloweth, the buck groaneth, the boar freameth; and whilst the hart had a Tail, the roe had a Single, the boar a Wreath, and the fox a Bush (not Brush be it noted) or Holy Water Sprinkle. Their amours (*e.g.* a fox went to clicketing), their young, their very excrements were dignified in a long array of special terms, the divisions and subdivisions of the deers' antlers being enough of themselves to gravel the tyro in woodcraft.

The peace of those precious animals was elaborately safeguarded, and it was specially forbidden "to haunt the forest" during the *Fence Moneth*, which was fifteen days before and after Midsummer. Most forests were surrounded by Purlieus, that is, territory which had been disafforested. Officers called Rangers patrolled this debateable territory to drive back the errant deer, and whilst the Purlieu-man (namely, the freeholder therein) might hunt on his own lands, he must call off his dogs if the beast once touched the forest. And every three years there was a special Drift of the forest, which was a sort of census of the venison. A man taken *With the Manner* (Main Ouverte), that is, in the act of doing for the deer, was attached without bail. The offender might thus be caught red-handed in four ways:—(1) in *Dog-Draw* he was chasing a wounded beast with hounds; (2) in *Stable-Stand* he was drawing his bow in ambush; (3) in *Back-Bare* he was carrying off his quarry; (4) in *Bloudy-Hand* he bore the red marks of his spoil. Divers statutes put a yet keener edge upon the common law, as that under Henry VII., whereby hunting in the forest at night with painted vizards was made a felony.

And what of the dogs? The forest freeholders might keep mastiffs for the protection of home and homestead; but a Court of Regards was held every three years for their Lawing or Expeditation. Thereat your mastiff was made to place one of his paws upon a billet of wood, "then one with a mallet, setting a chisel of three inches broad upon the three claws of his forefoot, at one blow doth smite them clean off." Other dogs of any size were summarily banished the precincts.

Royalty was ever jealous of these rights. A Fee-buck and a Fee-doe were allotted to every verderer yearly (but these were but wages in kind); and every lord of Parliament going or returning through the forest, on summons from the king, might take one or two beasts, but if no forester was at hand, he must sound his horn, lest the kill might seem done in secret. But all the king's horses and all the king's men could not quench English love of sport. Robin Hood and his merry band are but the glorified types of a very multitude who chased the deer night and day, for the forest stretched mile after mile over hill and dale, and the tall deer were fair to look on, and the taste of their flesh was as sweet to the wanderer and the outlaw as to the noble or the monarch; and the law, albeit cruel, was weak, and a touch of danger but gave zest to the pursuit. To take a later instance, was not Shakespeare himself the most illustrious of poachers? Not on such rovers but on the poor hard-working folk within the Regard did the forest laws press with cruel weight, and yet old Manwood highly extols their sweet reasonableness—"The king," he says, "wearied with his anxious care for the weal of his subjects, is given by law these forests that he may delight his eye at sight of the vert, and mind and body by the hunting of the wild beasts," and so he finds it in his heart to regret that in his day the forests were somewhat diminished. And since the sovereign's good is now the peoples' good, we may agree with him, though not for the same reason.

PAR NOBILE FRATRUM

JOHN DOE AND RICHARD ROE

Old English law being full of fictions, had pressing need ever and anon of imaginary characters to play imaginary parts. Sometimes a name was picked at random from the street, and Smith, you hear without surprise, was in great request, or, as those shadows came and went in couples, you find Richard Smith as often as not paired with William Styles. But your ancient scribe lusted after quaintness. He loved a jingle, so names like John Den and Richard Fen—rare in actual life—peopled his parchment, and strove for mastery in his mock combats. But his prime favourites were Doe and Roe, nor would he raise Den or Fen or any other ghost, excepting he had need of more than two. Here is a simple instance of their use. In early times a man who commenced an action had to give surety that he would go on with it; nowadays, if he discontinue, he must pay the costs of the other side, but costs, incredible as it may sound, were not always the necessary shadow, or perhaps the substance, of law; and hence the need for the pledge. Under Edward III. the practice went out of use, but the form of it, as legal forms are apt to do, lingered on for centuries in this style:—

Pledges of Prosecution { John Doe.
Richard Roe.

In the old Action of Ejectment the pair were most active. So strange were their gambols that even the lay world was impressed. In the early years of Victoria John and Richard were common butts of popular satire. Nothing seemed more gratuitous, more idly superfluous; but, turn to their history, and you find how important and how serviceable were the parts they once played.

One must begin far back. In early feudal times the cultivator of another's land was either a serf or a person of no importance, holding at his lord's will. The tenant's position improved with the times, leases were granted, and if their conditions were broken, a Writ of Covenant, as the form of action was called, secured him in possession, and gave him damages for his wrongs. But this action lay, as the technical term is, between the original parties alone; so that if he were turned out by a complete stranger, or by a person claiming through another grant of the same landlord, his remedy was merely pecuniary. In the time of Henry III. a writ was invented giving him full protection against anyone interfering under colour of another lease from his lord: but the case of an Ouster (or dispossession) by an utter stranger was not adequately provided for until the beginning of Edward III.'s reign, when the writ of *Ejectio Firmæ*, or ejectment, was adapted from the proceeding in trespass. It called upon the wrong-doer of every species to show why, "with force and arms," he had entered on and taken possession of the plaintiff's land. But, again, the result was only money damages: so that he was driven for relief to the equitable jurisdiction of the Chancellor, who, by injunctions and so forth, secured him in, or restored him to, possession of the very land itself. Presently the Common Law Courts took it ill that so much of their legitimate business should go elsewhere; and, at the end of the fifteenth century, they allowed the term itself, as well as damages for the Ouster, to be recovered under a Writ of Ejectment, and this remedy was held proper against every species of wrong-doer.

And if, not the tenant, but the landlord himself, were deprived of his property? or, if anyone not in possession claimed a piece of land as his freehold? These forms of procedure were not available, since they were personal actions, and a claimant to the freehold must proceed by a real action. These last were in early times the most important of all. But their forms were numerous and varied (the assizes of *morte d'ancestor* and *novel disseisin*, as they were called in old law French, were two of the best known), and their cumbersome and complicated technicalities were cause of much expense, irritation, and delay. At last it occurred to some ingenious, though forgotten, jurist so to twist this Writ of Ejectment, which had all the last improvements, as to make it available in an action for the recovery of the freehold. That was done in this way. A. was (let us suppose) the legal and rightful owner of an estate occupied in fact by B.; he entered on the land with C., to whom he, then and there, signed, sealed, and delivered a lease for the property in question; to them so engaged entered B., attracted by their manœuvring, and speedily kicked both into the boundary ditch. Here were all the materials for the action of ejectment, since C. might truly declare himself dispossessed *vi et armis* by B. from land whereof he held a lease from A. In this action the main point evidently was: Had A. a right to grant C. the lease? In other words, was A. the real owner of the land?

If the jury said "Yes," then judgment for possession followed for C., who, being merely the nominee of A., forthwith passed the property over to him. Improvements were speedily suggested. Actual ejection was like to prove unpleasant, so A. and C., instead of ostentatiously soliciting B.'s attention, took with them a confederate D., who, in a friendly and affable manner, performed the function of a chucker-out, and this casual ejector (as they named him) was made nominal defendant in the action wherein C. was nominal plaintiff. Lest B. should be condemned unheard, it was provided that the casual ejector must give him notice of the proceedings, whereupon he was let in to defend in place of D. This device was a brilliant practical success. Real actions pure and simple fell speedily into disuse, though it was not till 1833 that, with a few exceptions further tampered with in 1860, they were legally abolished.

The Commonwealth was a time of legal as well as political change. The Lord Protector had, with quaint emphasis, described the Court of Chancery as "an ungodly jumble," and Rolle, his Lord Chief Justice of the Upper Bench, before and since known as the King's Bench, laid violent hands on the action of ejectment. "What," urged he in effect, "was the use of actual entry, lease and ouster? Let all be held as done: so that the Court may apply itself at once to the real question at issue." Finally, the action was in name *Doe* against *Roe*, but the writ as a mere form was suppressed, and the first step was the declaration and notice to appear, both served on the real defendant or his tenant. The declaration stated that the land in question had been demised by A. (the real claimant) to John Doe; but that Richard Roe had entered thereon by force and arms and ejected him, "to the great damage of the said John Doe, and against the peace of our Lord the now King;" and that therefore he brought this action. To this there was appended a letter, signed "your loving friend Richard Roe," addressed to B., the real defendant, and informing him that the sender, hearing that he claimed the land, must now tell him that he (Richard), being sued "as a casual ejector only, and having no title to the same," he advised him (B.) to enter appearance as defendant, "otherwise I shall suffer judgment therein to be entered against me by default, and you will be turned out of possession." Now, to succeed in his action, the plaintiff must clearly prove four things—Title, Lease, Entry, and Ouster; and the three last he could not do, since they never happened. This little difficulty was got over by a consent rule: the Courts allowed B. to take Richard Roe's place as defendant, only on condition that he would confess those three things to have happened which never did happen: whereupon the real question of title alone remained.

So strangely had this action varied from its first use—which was to recover damages for wrongful possession of land—that in the result these were nominally estimated at a shilling; and if A. really wished to make B. disgorge the spoils of possession, he sued him again for Mesne Profits. Although the action was nominally "*Doe* against *Roe*," the cases are usually cited as "*Doe on the demise of A.*" (the real plaintiff) "against B." (the real defendant), and whilst John and Richard were the favourite styles, we have occasionally "*Good Title* against *Bad Title*": a comically impudent begging of the question at issue. If the outside public mocked these venerable figures, *par nobile fratrum*, the suitor did so at his peril. A certain Unitt (*temp.* George I.), being served with a copy of a Declaration in Ejectment, "pronounced contemptuous words on the delivery of it," and the judges in solemn conclave held that he was in contempt, and was deserving of punishment therefor. So the masque of shadows went on till 1852, when the Common Law Procedure Act removed an obstacle which lawyers had walked round for centuries, and consigned John Doe and Richard Roe to that limbo where so much legal rubbish lies buried under ever-thickening clouds of dust.

SANCTUARY

Your old-world lawyer was an ardent, if uncritical, antiquary. He began at the beginning, and where facts ran short his fancy filled up the blank. In discussing Sanctuary he started with the biblical cities of refuge. He had something to say of Romulus and the foundation of Rome. Geoffrey of Monmouth supplied him with the name of a sovereign—Dunwallo Molmutius to wit—who flourished in Druidical Britain (B.C. 500 it was said), under whom cities and even ploughs were arks of refuge for the despairing fugitive. It might have been objected that the ancient Britons had neither ploughs nor cities; but such criticism was not yet in the land. We touch firmer ground in the centuries immediately preceding the Conquest. In early English legislation churches safeguarded the criminal from hasty vengeance, and so allowed time to settle the money compensation payable for his offence. Sanctuary was among the privileges that the Conqueror conferred upon his foundation of Battle Abbey—one of many cases wherefrom the Norman lawyers built up a system for mediæval England.

That system was not always consistent or clear, but its main outlines were as follows:—sanctuaries were of two kinds—general, as all churches and churchyards; special, as St Martin's Le Grand and Westminster. No doubt these last had originally also a religious sanction. Such places were twice consecrate: Pope and King, the Canon and the Common Law united in their favour. They protected felons, but not those guilty of sacrilege or (some held) of treason. They were not properly for debtors, whose reception was nevertheless justified by an ingenious quibble. Imprisonment might endanger life, and therefore (so the learned argued) the runaway debtor must be received. A man took sanctuary thus—Having stricken (let us say) his fellow, he fled to the cathedral and knocked (with how trembling a hand!) at the door of the galilee. Over the north porch were two chambers where watchers abode night and day. On the instant the door swung open, and had scarce closed behind the fugitive when the galilee bell proclaimed to the town that another life was safe from them that hunted. Then the prior assigned him a gown of black cloth marked on the left shoulder with the yellow cross of St Cuthbert, and therewith a narrow space where he might lie secure of life, though ill at ease. So it was at Durham. At Westminster the sanctuary man bore the cross keys for a badge, and walked in doleful state before the abbot at procession times; and there were, no doubt, countless variations. A phrase of the time reveals how close the watch was now and again. Under Edward II. it was complained that the sanctuary man might not remove so much as a step beyond the precincts, *causâ superflui deponendi*, without being seized and haled to prison. He was fed and lodged in some rough sort for forty days, within which time he must confess his crime before the coroner at the churchyard gate, and so constitute himself the king's felon. Then he swore to abjure the realm. The coroner assigned him a port of embarcation (chosen by himself), whither he must hasten with bare head, carrying in his hand a cross, not departing, save in direst need, from the King's highway. He might tarry on the shore but a single ebb and flow of the tide, unless it were impossible to come by a ship, in which case he must wade up to his knees in the sea every day. He was thus protected for another forty days, when, if he could not find passage, he returned whence he came, to try his luck elsewhere.

He who refused to confess and abjure was not driven forth, but if, after much spiritual admonition, he still refused to conform, he had neither meat nor drink given him, and so was ended, if not mended. A man unjustly deprived of sanctuary could plead the right before his judges. It was a declinatory plea, and must be urged before he answered as to his guilt or innocence; it availed him nothing to do so after, for he was strung up forthwith. This system, however harsh, had two very plain advantages. It was a short and easy method with a rascal, and it powerfully made for scientific accuracy in pleading. If a fugitive were caught and condemned ere he "took Westminster," as the town phrase ran, it was no advantage for him to escape on the way to execution, inasmuch as he was promptly haled forth to the gallows. A curious case in the eighth of Edward II. perplexed the ancient student. A woman was condemned to death, but a jury of matrons had no doubt as to her condition, and she was reprieved. She escaped to sanctuary before the arrival of the hangman's cart, and when the gaoler dragged her out, the judges bade him put her back again, whereat the learned shook their heads, opining that hard cases make bad law, and the jade should have swung like other folk.

On the whole the privilege was strictly respected. For instance, the King's justices were wont to hold session in St Martin's Gate. They sat on the very border. The accused were placed on the other side of the street; a channel ran between them and their judges, and if they once got across *that* they claimed sanctuary, and all proceedings against them were annulled. And one sees the reason why Perkin Warbeck took such care "to squint one eye upon the crown and the other on the Sanctuary" (as Bacon curiously phrases it); yet the great case of Beckett is there to show that nothing was absolutely sacred in these violent years. Nor does it stand alone. In 1191, Jeffrey, Archbishop of York, and son of Henry II., was seized at the altar of St Martin's Priory, Dover; and dragged, episcopal robes and all, through dirty streets to the Castle: this, too, by order of William Longchamp, Bishop of Ely, and Papal Legate. In 1378, Archbishop Sudbury complained in Parliament that one Robert Hawley had been slain at the high altar even while the priest was saying a mass. It was rumoured indeed that one Thurstian, a Knight, chasing a sanctuary man with drawn sword, was of a sudden stricken with grievous ailments. But this and other like stories did not deter the citizens of London (*circa* 1349) from assembling at supper time in a great crowd, and dragging forth a soldier who had escaped on the way from Newgate to Guildhall, where he was being taken for trial. In another case (*temp.* Henry VI.), where a youth had taken sanctuary after having foully slain a kind mistress, the good women about St Martin's broke in and despatched him with their distaffs. Of those who took sanctuary to good purpose the most famous was Elizabeth, widow of Edward IV., who, in 1471, registered herself a sanctuary woman in Westminster, and there sat, in Sir Thomas More's phrase, "Alow in the rushes." But you have read the tragic story in Shakespeare. And in a later age "beastly Skelton" (as Pope will have him), from that same Westminster safely lampooned the mighty Wolsey, though for that he needs must live and die there.

To catalogue the evils of the sanctuary system were to show lack of historical sympathy, nay, even of humour. The former days were not as these; it had its place with the shrine and the pilgrimage, the knight errant, and the trial by ordeal in the strange economy of a vanished world. As the times grew modern its practical inconvenience was felt for the first time. Yet the occasion of the first assault on the privilege of sanctuary was one where the benefits were conspicuous, and the assailant had the worst of motives. It was the case just noted of Edward IV.'s widow; she had the young Duke of York as yet safe with her. Her enemies were at a loss for the moment, and Buckingham, then the sworn ally of Richard of Gloucester, took occasion in the Privy Council to attack her place of refuge. "There were two chief plague-spots in London," he snarled: "one at the elbows of the city (Westminster), the other in the very bowels thereof (St Martin's le Grand). These places were the refuge of theeves, murtherers, and malitious, heynous traytors! nay," he added, "men's wives ran hither with their husbands' plate, and say they dare not abide their husbands for beating," with more to the same effect. Had not Elizabeth yielded, Westminster might have witnessed a violation as affecting as that of Canterbury.

Under Henry VIII. the old order was broken up, and sanctuary law, like much else, was changed and amended again and again. First, all special places save Wells, Westminster, and six others, lost the privilege. Divers classes of criminals —as traitors, and pirates (and afterwards) Egyptians—were formally rendered incapable of its enjoyment. Before the sanctuary man abjured the realm he was burned on the crown of the thumb "with the signe of an A," and if he did not depart on the instant, he had no further protection. But it occurred to over-anxious legislators that such a fugitive might carry beyond seas precious hints of the mysteries of trade or politics, or that, making as if for the nearest port, he might but proceed to infest another place. So he was ordered to abjure the liberty of the realm, but not the realm itself; and being branded, was confined under a governor in one or other of the sanctuaries. Whenever he ventured forth—as he might in the daytime—he must wear the prescribed badge of the refuge. He dare carry no weapon save a meat-knife, and that but at meal-times. He must likewise answer to the daily roll-call. If he committed another felony—and crimes done *sub spe redeundi* had been a sore grievance of late—he was to lose his rights. The governor was empowered to hold courts for debt and minor offences within his bounds. And so "the sanctuary person abjured," as the Tudor lawyers phrased him, spent the last days of his evil life. I need not dwell on minor tinkerings of the system under Henry's children. In 1623 the Statute 21 James I., c. 28, s. 7 made a legal end of the right of sanctuary.

The last of our story is not yet. Certain places still assumed the right of giving shelter against civil process. When the bailiffs invaded the liberty, the whole population forthwith set on, and pommelled them so lustily that they were fortunate if they escaped sound in limb. The precincts of Whitefriars and the Savoy were the worst places in London. The first, renowned in slang, nay, in literature, as Alsatia, because (some explained) it neighboured the Temple on the East, as Alsace did France, was a base and villainous Bohemia. Ram Alley (now Mitre Court), a local Lombard

Street, Salisbury Court (now Salisbury Square) were its chief ways, though probably all between Fleet Street and the river, which was not the Temple, held of this lawless republic. A bully or bravo, or squire of Alsatia was a cant name for a penniless and violent fellow of the time. He is pictured by Otway in his *Soldier's Fortune* with flopping hat pinned up on one side, with a tawdry weather-beaten peruke, dirty linen, and a long scandalous iron sword jangling at his heels. The sheriff with the *posse comitatus* did on occasion raid Alsatia, but his prey, if too weak to fight, had ever timely warning to escape by land or water to some other like burrow. *The Fortunes of Nigel* tells as much of the place as the general cares to know, and there is much curious matter mined out by the zealous antiquary as to other like places of refuge in the capital. Thus Fullwood's, sometime Fuller's Rents, was related to Gray's Inn as Alsatia to the Temple. In 1673 the gentlemen of that ancient house so far forgot themselves as to engage in "pumping" some bailiffs who attempted to take goods from out the Rents upon an execution. "They were charged with a body of thirty lusty bailiffs," and a "strong ryot" ensued. Possibly they recollected that their most illustrious fellow-member, "broad-browed Verulam," had taken refuge there some sixty years before, a circumstance which gave my Lord Coke occasion to "gall the kibe"—as indeed he never lost any chance to do—of his great contemporary. Then there was the mint in Southwark, whereto an ex-poet laureate, "poor Nahum Tate," as Dr. Johnson calls him, was driven by extreme poverty. Pope's cruel satire pictures it half Grub Street half Bedlam, the last refuge of the hack and the poetaster. The Clink and Deadman's place are now forgotten, whilst Baldwin's Gardens and the Minories have a more commonplace reputation.

About a century after James's Act, Parliament again interfered, and professed to strip the "pretended privileged places" of every shred of exemption, but it required two other statutes, the 9 Geo. I. c. 28, 1722, and the 11 Geo. I. c. 22, 1724, to make the law's process as effectual there as elsewhere.

TRIAL BY ORDEAL

Before the Conquest, and for long after, local justice in England was administered by two courts—that of the Hundred and that of the Shire. The first nominally consisted of the freeholders of the district, but the real business was done by a Committee of Twelve. The second was made up of the chief men of the district, and representatives from each township; but here, again, the work was left to a select few. If a man were charged with (say) theft before either court, he was tried in a fashion vastly different from that obtaining to-day. The complainant was sworn on the holy relics: "By the Lord I accuse not this man either for hatred, or for envy, or for unlawful lust of gain." This solemn accusation made out a *primâ facie* case against the suspect, who instantly rebutted oath with oath. "By the Lord I am guiltless, both in deed and in counsel of this charge." Then he produced twelve compurgators, who swore by the Lord, "The oath is clean and unperjured which this man hath sworn"; then the prisoner went free. These compurgators were witnesses to character. Their testimony had no reference to the particular facts of the case; they simply alleged their belief in accused's innocence, but sometimes their oath "burst" (as the curious technical phrase ran), that is, he could not find compurgators, or those he produced said little good of him; or he was a stranger of whom nothing was known; or a Welshman whose veracity has never been an article of faith; or the accused was caught with his booty; or was a woman; or the charge was peculiarly odious, as treason, or witchcraft; then in all these cases there was an appeal to the *Judicium Dei,* the Creator was called upon to prove beyond dispute the guilt or innocence of the accused.

Trial by Ordeal was more ancient than the Church itself. There are traces of it in the Old Testament; it is discussed in great detail in the Laws of Manu; a famous passage in the *Antigone* (verses 264-267) reveals it as well known to the Greeks, and before Augustine came, or St Columba preached, it prevailed in some form or other in Britain. Yet the higher ecclesiastical powers continually thundered against it, and finally brought about its disuse. There were several varieties, but many forms were common to all. First, there was the ordeal of cold water, chiefly reserved for the baser fellow.

As a preliminary the accused submitted to a fast of three days, during which he was watched by a priest, then he was taken to church to hear Mass; and was adjured by Father, Son, and Holy Ghost, by the gospels and relics of the saints, by everything held most sacred, not to partake of communion if he were guilty. Next came the *adjuratio aquæ*, wherein the water was enjoined to cast him forth if he were guilty, but to receive him into its depths if innocent. And now, having been stripped, he kissed the Book and the Cross, was sprinkled with holy water and was cast in, to float if he were guilty, to sink if he were not. But there was the rub—how about death by suffocation? Sir James Stephen suggests that it was all a mode of happy despatch! Or (one fancies) it might be an elementary form of the famous verdict "not guilty, but don't do it again," with the chance of doing it again effectually provided against. On the other hand, a recipe for immersion in a thirteenth century MS. of the Monastery of Becca reduces the proceedings to the level of farce. The hands of the accused were tied, and a rope was put round his waist; "and let a knot be made in the rope as high up as the longest hair of the man's head will reach, and then in this way let him be gently lowered into the water; and if he sinks down to the knot, let him be pulled out as innocent; if not, let him be adjudged guilty." How *not* to sink under such conditions? The practice of testing witches by throwing them, securely tied, into the nearest pond was clearly a survival of this form of ordeal.

In the ordeal by hot water the accused, plunging his hand to the wrist in the boiling fluid, brought forth a stone suspended therein by a cord. (This was the Single Ordeal, and it became the Triple when the plunge was up to the elbow.) The arm was done up in bandages not to be removed till after three days; if the scald had healed the man was innocent, if it still festered he was guilty. In the ordeal by hot iron, a piece of red-hot metal was carried a distance of nine feet; it was then dropped and the hand was bandaged as already set forth. A knight had to thrust his fist into a glowing gauntlet; another form was a walk with naked feet over a sequence of red-hot ploughshares. We have a picturesque circumstantial and absolutely untrustworthy monkish account of how Emma, mother of Edward the Confessor, being suspected of an all too intimate acquaintance with Alwyn, Bishop of Winchester, underwent this trial. She took nine steps for herself and five for the Bishop, fixing her eyes the while on heaven. "When shall we reach these ploughshares?" queried she. How agreeable a surprise to find her little promenade already past and done with! No need to swathe *her* feet, the red-hot iron had marked them not at all!

The last mode was the *Corsnæd*, or Cursed Morsel—a piece of barley-bread (or cheese), one ounce in weight. This "Creature of Sanctified Bread" was adjured, in terms terrible enough to make the sinner quake, to stick in the guilty throat, and cause the guilty jaws to be clenched and locked up. If in spite of all it went softly down, who dared to refuse belief in the man's innocence? It was chiefly for the clergy, and from every point of view must have been the most agreeable of the three, though a legend as untrustworthy as that of Emma ascribes to it the death of Earl Godwin, father of Harold. As he sat at meat with Edward the Confessor, the king brought up an old scandal about his brother's murder, "May God cause this morsel to choke me," passionately exclaimed the earl, "if I am guilty of the crime!" Edward blessed the bread; Godwin made an effort to swallow, choked and died. "Take away that dog," said the monarch in what would seem an outburst of savage glee. This was on April 15th, 1053, thirteen years before the Conquest. Godwin in truth died of a fit. It soon was the policy of the monkish chroniclers to write down the national party of which he had been the head, a fact which explains the fable were it worth serious examination. More interesting to note the survival of the rite in the still current rustic formula, "May this bit choke me if I lie!" If the ordeal proved a man guilty, the punishment was fine, death or outlawry, but even if he escaped, the Assize of Clarendon (1164) ordered that, in certain cases, he should abjure the realm. By that time compurgation was gone; in 1215 the Lateran Council issued a solemn decree against Trial by Ordeal; and soon after it had vanished from English law. There is a curious reference to it in the State Trials as late as 1679. John Govan, a Jesuit priest, was indicted in that year at the Old Bailey for an alleged share in the Popish Plot. With some hesitation he claimed the right of Trial by Ordeal as an ecclesiastical privilege of a thousand years' standing, but Scroggs and North peremptorily refused to listen to his plea. "We have no such law now," said the latter. Sir James Stephen assures us that the formula, "By God and by my country," wherein, till 1827, a prisoner must answer the question how he would be tried, sets forth a memory of it.

Of the customs akin to Trial by Ordeal only one can find mention here. It was held that if the murderer touched, nay, even approached, the body of his victim, the wounds gushed forth blood, thus in *Richard the Third*, "dead Henry's wounds" are seen "to open their congealed mouths and bleed afresh" as Gloucester draws near the bier. And according to one of the picturesque legends of English history, when Richard the Lion-Heart encountered at Fontevrault his father's body, the blood gushed from the nostrils of the dead king, a proceeding which, as Richard's offence was at the worst but unkindness, showed a somewhat excessive sensibility on the part of the royal clay. The oddest and latest case of all is from Scotland. In 1688 Philip Stanfield was tried for parricide at Edinburgh; one count of the indictment stated how his father's body had bled at his sacrilegious touch. The Lord Advocate, Sir George Mackenzie of Rosehaugh, the "Bluidy Mackenzie" of covenanting legend and tradition, conducted the prosecution, and philosophic and cultured jurist as he was, he yet dwelt with much emphasis on the portentous sign. There was no lack of more satisfactory if more commonplace evidence, and young Stanfield assuredly merited the doom in the end meted out to him.

WAGER OF BATTLE

Judicial combat is a fascinating yet perplexing subject, having many side-issues whereupon the writer must sternly refrain. The case of David and Goliath was gravely urged (a.d. 867) as a precedent to Pope Nicholas I., and by him disdainfully put aside. The thing itself was unknown in Roman law, though the old legend of the Horatii and Curatii was part of its lore. But it was of the essence of chivalry, and the duel and the prize-fight were its legitimate offspring. "Where the hazel grew," so Mr George Nelson, our chief modern authority, picturesquely defines its region, but our attention here must be limited to England. That it was *not* with us before the Conquest moves Bishop Stubbs to something of the scholar's mild amazement. The Normans, it seems clear, brought it with them from their continental home. A native accused of a serious crime by one of the invaders was tried by ordeal of battle, but a Norman had choice of the oath as well, and it was also used to decide which of the claimants should have a disputed piece of land. After the legal reforms of Henry II., it became an alternative proceeding in a limited class of actions. These were the Writ of Right (the most solemn method of trying title to land), accusations of murder, and treason. It had place only in appeals, in actions, that is to say, brought not in the king's name, but by an interested subject here called the Appellor, against whom the accused or Appellee might offer to prove his innocence by his body. The Appellor must accept the challenge unless he were maimed by age or wound. Likewise he could "Oust the Battle" (*i.e.* prove this mode of trial improper) if the accused were caught red-handed. The parties exchanged gloves, and gave pledges or wads (*vadiare bellum*); whence came Wager of Battle, afterwards the technical term for the whole process. In civil cases, if the litigants came to terms, the judge exacted a fine, called the Concord, while he who fought and lost must pay the mulct of Recusancy. In criminal matters he who resisted not till the stars shone forth was branded as Recreant or Craven and was forthwith strung up, and all his goods were declared forfeit. The Charters of Exemption purchased from overlord or king show how hateful the system was to the old English citizen. Henry I. enacted for a consideration that no Londoner should do battle, and in due course the men of Winchester, Lincoln, and Northampton obtained the like privilege.

The story of Leicester is worth the telling. In the time of Henry I. Earl Robert of Mellant ruled the town. It chanced that two burghers, Nicholas and Jeffrey, waged battle on a plea of land. For nine long hours they mauled each other with varying fortune, when one of them took to flight, and staggered, all unwitting, on the edge of a pit. The other saw his danger, and remembered that they twain were kinsmen. "'Ware o' the pit," he shouted; "turn back, lest thou fall therein." The spectators so lustily roared their approval, that the Earl heard it in his castle, and he, after due enquiry, granted that in time coming twenty-four jurors of Leicester should determine all civic disputes. One strange product of Trial by Combat was the Approver: a rascal who turned king's evidence, and fought with his late companions. Sometimes he accused other malefactors, and if he came off victor in five combats he was released, and banished the country. This system fell into gross abuse, for the Approver, greedy of freedom or hush-money, appealed honest men right and left. In the chronicle of William Gregory the Skinner (1456) we have an account of a duel fought by one Thomas Whitehorne, a criminal, caught in the New Forest, and lodged in prison at Winchester, where he remained for about three years, fighting ever and anon. "And that fals and untrewe peler (= Appelar) hadde of the Kynge every day 1d. ob." At last a proposed victim retorted the lie in his throat, and said that "he wold prove hyt with hys handys and spende hys lyfe and blode a-pone hys fals body." Then the judge "fulle curtesly informed this sympylle man" that "he and the peler moste be clothyed all in whyte schepys leter." Also each must have a stave of green ash, three feet long, the point thereof "a horne of yryn i-made lyke unto a rammy's horne;" and if these ash-plants broke, then they "moste fight with hyr handys, fystys, naylys, tethe, fete, and leggys." Moreover, they must strive fasting on the "moste sory and wrechyd greene about the town;" but "Huyt ys to schamfulle to reherse alle the condycyons of thys foule conflycte." And we must follow Gregory's precept rather than his example.

The Appellee, asking for inquiry as to his character, was reported "a fyscher and tayler of crafte," and therewith the "trewyste laborer and the moste gentellyte." The peler, with brazen insolence, offered *his* character for inspection. There was much dubiety as to where and how he had lived when at large, but "Hange uppe Thome Whythorne" was the response of every reference he tendered. At last the day came. The Appellee, as became an innocent man, told his beads, and prayed long and earnestly, and wept full sore, and all present prayed for and with him. The "fals peler" scoffed thereat. "Thou fals trayter," yelled he; "why arte thou soo longe in fals bytter beleve?" The defendant's sole answer was so lusty a thwack that his staff flew all to pieces. Thereupon the peler's stave was taken away from *him*; "ande thenn they wente togedyr by the neckys," so using teeth and fist, "that the lethyr of clothing and fleshe was alle to rente in many placys of hyr bodys." It fared ill at first with the "meke innocent." His opponent had him down on the ground, and near choked the life out of him. But presently the meek one got up on his knees, and (the combat not being under Queensberry rules), "toke that fals peler by the nose with hys tethe, and put hys thombe in hys yee, that the peler cryde owte ande prayde hym of marcy, for he was fals unto God and unto hym." The peler's subsequent record is of the briefest, but, one is thankful to add, of the most edifying description. "And thenn he was confessyd and hanggyd, of whose soule God ha' marcy." Amen. "*Victus est et susp*," so for epitaph wrote the official scribe against his name. And the exchequer parchments knew him and his "*1d. ob. per diem*" no more.

The Champion, now but the shadow of a name, was a nobler offshoot of the system. Originally a witness, he was finally indispensable in civil cases wherein—for a legal reason not here to be discussed—the parties themselves must not engage. He was the proper advocate for churchmen, for women, and for the Crown; and his last appearance for royalty was in 1820, at the coronation of George IV. The Dymocks have held the manor of Scrivelsby in Lincolnshire for centuries by this tenure, and possibly their representative claimed a part in the pageant on the two subsequent occasions, but to have him ride up Westminster Hall in full armour and clang his gauntlet on the floor (as he did of old) would have savoured too much of Drury Lane pantomime for the taste of a cynical age. The Champion's dress and bearing were minutely ordered. His head (*e.g.*) was shaven, but whether this was to give no hold to his foe, or to fulfil some old superstition, is still in debate among the learned. In the end he was usually a hireling, which fact may very well have accentuated the absurdity of the system. At any rate, towards the close of the thirteenth century it was only kept alive by the approvers. Then Chivalry came with its Treason Duel, and by the time of Richard II. the Chivalry Court was in full swing. Its forms, mainly imported, were after this wise. Upon the accusation and the exchange of gloves, time and place were assigned for the duel, and here the lists were set and staked. There were two gates, and hard by each a pavilion—one eastward for the appellant, and the other westward for the defendant. To the south was the judge's seat; and right and left were benches for the high-born, while the commons were made free of the unenclosed field. Near the judge an altar was decked with relics; and not far off there stood a gibbet and a scaffold. Men-at-arms were stationed between the palisades. There were heralds in gay tabards, a priest in full canonicals stood at the altar—but it were wearisome to enumerate all the officials.

The trial was held not less than forty days after the challenge; and the time being come, the heralds demanded silence; and the appellant was summoned three times by voice and by sound of trumpet. As he marched forward he was addressed by the Constable, "Who art thou, and wherefore comest thou armed to the door of these lists?" His answer given, he was taken to his pavilion, and afterwards was made to swear on the altar that his cause was just. The other did in like fashion. Then the pavilions were replaced by chairs whereon the combatants might take an occasional rest. Napkins holding a loaf and a bottle of water were hung on opposite ends of the lists. The marshal cried three times "*Laissez les aller*," and the pair went at it. Far better death than defeat. If either yielded, the marshal cried "Hoo," to declare the combat at an end. Then the wretch was taken to the scaffold on which his shield was hung reversed, his sword was broken, and his spurs hacked from his heels. He was now taken to the church where a mass for the dead was sung over him, and at last he was haled to the gibbet where the hangman claimed his prey.

This is the form of judicial combat that caught the fancy of our great writers. In Chaucer's *Knight's Tale* there is the elaborate set to between Palamon and Arcite. In Shakespeare's *Richard II.* there is the fiasco of Norfolk and Hereford. In *Lear* we have the fight to the death between Edmund and Edgar, and "every schoolboy knows" The Templar's duel in *Ivanhoe*.

Chivalry passed, yet not the half-forgotten wager of battle. A claim so to determine a civil dispute was made in 1571, to the great perplexity of the lawyers. Elaborate preparations were made, but the case was settled in other fashion. Under James I. bills were introduced into Parliament to abolish it, but they fell through, and in 1774, at the beginning of the North American troubles, when it was proposed to punish the New Englanders by depriving them of the appeal of murder, Dunning, afterwards Lord Ashburton, described it as that great pillar of the Constitution. Burke concurred, and the motion was lost. Perhaps they have it yet in the States, at least Dr Cooper, in editing, in 1857, the statutes at large of South Carolina, treats Wager of Battle as an existing fact. In England the end came in dramatic fashion. In May 1817 Mary Ashford—a young woman of Langley in Warwickshire, was found drowned under suspicious circumstances. A certain Abram Thornton was suspected of the murder; he was tried and acquitted, but there was much evidence against him, and he had played so ill a part in a horrid though vulgar tragedy that the relatives of the dead girl cast about to carry the matter further. Now, an old act provided that no acquittal by jury should bar an appeal of murder, so William Ashford, Mary's brother, appealed Thornton in the Court of King's Bench. He was attached, and when called upon pleaded "Not guilty, and am ready to defend the same by my body." He then threw down his glove on the floor of the Court. It was a curious turn; for no doubt men thought that he would put himself upon the country, and stand a second trial by jury. There was much legal argument (set forth at great length in the reports of the time), for the prosecuting counsel tried hard to "oust his battle," but to no purpose, and in the end Thornton was set free. In 1819, two years after the drowning of Mary Ashford, the Appeal of Murder Act (59 Geo. III. c. 46) abolished the last remnant of Wager of Battle.

THE PRESS-GANG

Smollett, Galt, Marryatt, and the other naval novelists, not those well-nigh forgotten Dry-as-dusts whose works encumber the back shelves of our law libraries, are the authorities for the press-gang of popular imagination. The sea-port invaded, the house surrounded at dead of night by man-o'-war's men with stout cudgels, and by naval officers with cutlasses; the able-bodied mariner knocked down *first* and *then* bid stand in the king's name; the official shilling thrust into his reluctant palm before he is hauled off in irons—who has not devoured with joy this wild romance, with its tang of the sea, its humour and rough frolic, the daring and exciting prelude to much more daring and more exciting achievements? But how far can we trust these entertaining authors? And what was the legal status of the press-gang?

We are like to get nearest the truth in a law case with its official documents and sifted evidence and considered decision. The trial of one Alexander Broadfoot for the murder of one Calahan is the best available. In the April of 1774 H.M.S. *Mortar* lay at anchor off Bristol. The captain held a warrant of impressment, but he could delegate his authority only to a commissioned officer, whose name must be inserted in his order; and the only one aboard was the lieutenant. On the 25th the ship's boat was sent down Channel, *with neither captain nor lieutenant* to look for men. She had no luck till evening, when she came across the *Bremen Factor*, a homeward bound merchantman, still some leagues from port, but beating thitherward up Channel. The man-o'-war's men having boarded her, were proceeding to search the hold, when they were confronted by Broadfoot, the boatswain, armed to the teeth. He demanded what they came for. "For you and your comrades," was the plain and honest, though no doubt irritating answer. "Keep back, I have a blunderbuss loaded with swan shot," said Broadfoot, levelling his piece. The press-gang stopped. "Where is your lieutenant?" he went on. (Evidently this boatswain knew a little of the law.) "He is not far off," was the evasive answer, showing that the man's acts and words had impressed his assailants. Did Broadfoot grasp the fact that they were trespassers? At any rate, he let fly, killed Calahan on the spot, and wounded two others. He was tried at Bristol, and acquitted of the capital charge—for the action of the man-o'-war's men was plainly irregular; but he was found guilty of manslaughter, for that he had used more force than was necessary. Another case is that of Robert Goldswain, a small freeholder at Marlow, in Bucks. In the March of 1778 he was a bargeman on the Thames, engaged in carrying timber to the king's yard; with a protection order from the Navy Board to him by name so long as he should continue in that service. But these were troubled times, the French had just declared for the revolted American colonists and our war-ships were frightfully undermanned; so, on the 16th of March, the Admiralty fixed the next night for a general press on the Thames, with direction to seize—despite protection orders—on all sailors and watermen whatsoever, saving and excepting merchant skippers and men exempted by special acts. Goldswain was in the net, and was passed from ship to ship down to the Nore, where his captors were overtaken by an order from the Court requiring a return to a writ of Habeas Corpus issued on his behalf. Counsel's argument for the Admiralty—that the device of first issuing protection orders to lure sea and watering men from their lurking-places, and then pouncing on them under the authority of a general press, was excellent—did not commend itself to the Court, which, in the battle over poor Goldswain's body, suspected some antagonism between the Admiralty and the Naval Board. In the end my lords gave way, and Marlow received again her ravished freeholder.

During the strain and stress of our eighteenth century war-making, when we had every need of seamen to man our battle-ships, and could not afford the market price for them, there was much impressment, and through frequent appeals to the courts the law on the subject was exactly determined. It was a prerogative of the Crown, a remnant of larger rights which at one time took in soldiers and ships, or their equivalent in cash (Hampden's famous trial scarce needs mention); it could not be justified (it was allowed) by reason, but only by public necessity. On command of the king all sea and river-faring men were liable to naval service in time of war. The right to impress was founded on immemorial usage, for, though given by no statute, it was recognised by many. It was so held on the authority of a case in Queen Elizabeth's reign: the sole customary exception was a ferryman; but merchant captains were in practice likewise allowed to go free. Only in Charles I.'s reign, when all the Crown prerogatives were jealously overhauled, was there any serious questioning of its legality, but it was exercised by the Commonwealth as well as by the Monarchy. Given up in fact some fifty years since, it has never been so in law. You find in Horner's *Crown Practice* (1844) a form of *Habeas Corpus ad subjiciendum* for impressed men, with the comment that it is little needed now.

Of the enormous number of commissions and statutes relating to impressment, an example taken here and there must suffice. The acts express amazement and virtuous indignation at mariners unwilling to serve. One (*temp.* Henry VII.) sets forth that such as are chosen, and have received their wages, shall, if they give leg-bail, be amerced in double, and go to prison for a year—when they are caught. Another (*temp.* Philip and Mary) reproves the Thames watermen who, in pressing time, "do willingly and obstinately withdraw, hide, and convey themselves into secret places and outcovers; and, after the said time of pressing is o'erpassed, return to their employments." After the Revolution an attempt was made to establish a naval reserve by means of a voluntary register, and so do away with impressment, but this was a complete failure. Then, to foster the coal and other trades, certain exceptions were granted; and still later, sailors in outward bound merchantmen were exempted because of the hardship inflicted on their employers (the hardship of the sailor impressed in sight of port after a long voyage was not considered). When a warship fell in with a merchantman on the high seas she impressed what men she would. British sailors found on board American vessels were hauled out forthwith, and this was one cause of the War of 1812.

Press-gang stories, more or less authentic, are numerous. Here are samples which serve to show that the searchers did not nicely discriminate between those who were and were not legally subject to impressment. A well-dressed man was seized. He protested that he was a gentleman of position. "The very boy we want," gleefully replied his captors; "for we've such a set of topping blackguards aboard the tender, that we wanted a gentleman to teach 'em manners." Sham press-gangs for the black-mailing of honest citizens were common. In one case a couple had given all their money to go free, when the real gang coming up made booty of both parties, and had them aboard in no time. The quarrymen at Denny Bowl, sixty strong, were heard to brag in their cups what *they* would do did the press-gang dare to molest *them*, whereupon "three merry girls" got into breeches, put cockades in their hats, took sword and pistol, and advanced, when the quarrymen ran like hares. And to conclude, there is the legend of the gang that raided "The Cock and Rummer" in Bow Street. They seized the cook. The customers, fearing for their dinner, or themselves, rushed to the rescue. Long the strife hung dubious, when the constable (he ought to have been a Bow Street runner) stalked in. The gang, with a fine sense of humour, let the cook go, seized *him*, and away at a great rate, though not fast enough to get clear.

SUMPTUARY LAWS

"Act of Parliament" is a term apt to mislead. To-day it is enforced by so powerful a machinery that practice conforms to precept; but in mediæval England much law was dead letter. Statutes were often mere admonitions; they expressed but an ideal, a pious intention. This was specially true of the Sumptuary Laws, whereby the dress and food of the king's subjects were nicely regulated. If you turn over a book of costumes you find that man's attire has varied more than woman's. The sorts and conditions of men were marked by rigid lines. This fact was shown forth in their dress, and that again re-acted on their modes of thought and habits of life. "Men's apparel," says Edmund Spenser, "is commonly marked according to their condition, and their conditions are often-times governed by their garment, for the person that is gowned is by his gown put in mind of gravity, and also restrained from lightness by the very unaptness of his Tweed." Of old time man's dress was rich and varied, but how to catch its vanished effect? In Courts of Justice there is still the splendid, if occasional, bravery of the judge. See the same man in private, gaze on divinity disrobed, and the disenchantment measures for you what is lost in the splendid garb of other days. In mediæval Europe the Church first condemned a too ornate appearance. Thus, under our early Norman Kings, long hair was much in vogue. In 1104 Bishop Serlo, preaching before Henry I. and his Court in Normandy, attacked this fashion roundly, compared his hearers to "filthy goats," and moved them by his eloquence to tears of contrition. He saw and seized that softer hour. Descending from the pulpit he then and there clipped the polls of them that heard him till he must fain sheath his shears for lack of argument. This rape of the locks was followed by a royal edict against long hair. Alas! for this story. Rochester Cathedral still bears the effigies of Henry and Maud his queen; each is adorned even as Absalom, and Time, whilst it has mauled their faces in cruel fashion, has with quaint irony preserved intact those stone tresses.

Two centuries pass ere the Sumptuary Laws proper begin. The 10 Edward III. c. 3 (1336) ordered that no man was to have more than two courses at dinner, nor more than two kinds of meat, with potage in each course; but on eighteen holidays in the year the lieges might stuff at will. Next Parliament common folk were forbidden to wear furs; but the 37 Edward III. was the great session for such work, made needful (it was thought) by the sudden increase of luxury from the plunder of the French wars. Some half-dozen Acts prescribed to each rank, from peers to ploughmen, its wear; nay, the very price of the stuff was fixed; whilst all wives were to garb themselves according to their husbands' means—a pious wish, repeated a century afterwards, in an Act of the Scots James II. The veils of the baser sort were not to cost more than 12d. apiece: embroidery or silk was forbidden to servants, and these were to eat of flesh or fish but once a day. Cloth merchants were to make stuff enough, and shopkeepers to have stock enough, to supply the anticipated demand. Such apparel as infringed the statute was forfeit to the king. The knight's dress will serve for sample of what was required. It was to be cloth of silver, with girdles reasonably embellished with silver, and woollen cloth of the value of six marks the piece. Under Richard II. monstrous sleeves were much affected. A monkish scribe inveighs bitterly against these "pokys, like bag-pipes." Some hung down to the knees; yea, even to the feet. Servants were as bad as their masters! When potage is brought to table, "the sleeves go into them and get the first taste." Nay, they are "devil's receptacles," since anything stolen is safely lodged therein. And so a statute of the time prohibited any man below a banneret from wearing large hanging sleeves, open or closed.

The fashion changed to *dagges*, a term explained by the 8th of Henry IV., which forbade "gown or garment cut or slashed into pieces in the form of letters, rose-leaves, and posies of various kinds, or any such devices." The fantastic peaked shoes of the fifteenth century, sometimes only held up by a chain from the girdle, were fair mark for the lawgiver, and under Edward IV. no less person than a lord was allowed peaks exceeding two inches. An Act in the same reign banned the costly head-gear of women. Henry VIII. saw to men's garb as well as their beliefs. His first Parliament forbade costly apparel, and there is preserved in the Record Office a letter from Wolsey enclosing to the King, at his request, the Act of Apparel, with an abstract, for examination and correction. Exemptions were not unknown: thus, in 1517, Henry Conway of Bermondsey obtained license to wear "camlet, velvet, and sarcenet, satin and damask, of green, black, or russet colour in his clothing." Under Queen Mary common folk who wore silk on "hat, bonnet, girdle, scabbard, hose, shoes, or spur-leathers," were grievously amerced. Under Elizabeth the regulations were numberless: thus there is an act for "uttering of caps, and for true making of hats and caps." No one was to engage in this business unless he had been "a prentice or covenant servant" by the space of seven years. No one under the degree of knight was to wear a cap of velvet. But these were not pure sumptuary regulations: they were for protection of home industries. A statute of the previous reign had declared that no man was to buy more than twelve hats or caps, be it out of this realm; and a previous Act of Elizabeth had strangely provided that if anyone sold foreign apparel on credit for longer than eight days to persons not having £3000 a year he should be without legal remedy against his debtor.

On the 15th June 1574, an elaborate proclamation complained of "the wasting and undoying of a great number of young gentlemen" who were "allured by the vayne shewe of those thyngs." A schedule was appended in which the costumes prescribed for all sorts and conditions of men were set forth. In the Star Chamber on June 12th, 1600, my Lord Keeper gravely admonished the judges to look to all sorts of abuses—"Solicitors and pettifoggers," "Gentlemen that leave hospitality and housekeeping and hide in cities and borough towns;" "Masterless men that live by their sword and their wit, meddlers in princes' matters and libellers," and last, but not least, "to the vanity and excess of woman's apparel." All was in vain, if we are to believe the fierce invective of Stubb's *Anatomie of Abuses*. "There is now," he groans, "such a confused mingle-mangle of apparel, and such preposterous excess thereof as every one is permitted to flaunt it out in whatever apparel he listeth himself, or can get by any kind of means." It was horrible to hear that shirts were sold at £10 a piece, and "it is a small matter now to bestow twenty nobles, ten pound, twenty pound, forty pound, yea, a hundred pound, of one pair of breeches (God be merciful to us!)" After this aught else were anti-climax, and so for the women he can only say they were worse than the men. A new order of things came in with the next reign, for the act Jac. I. c. 25, sec. 45, repealed at one stroke all statutes against apparel. In Scotland they kept up the game some time longer, but one need not pursue the subject there, though a curious statute of the Scots James II. (1457) must have a word. It provided that "na woman cum to Kirk nor mercat with her face mussled that she may nocht be kenn'd under the pain of escheit of the curchie" (forfeiture of the hood). In Ireland there was a law (says Spenser) which "forbiddeth any to weare theyre beardes on the upper lip and none under the chinn:" another "which putteth away saffron shirtes and smockes," and so forth; but these were of English importation.

In the North American colonies sumptuary legislation has a history of its own. In Massachusetts an edict of September 1639, declaims against the "much waste of the good creatures (not the tipplers, but the tipple) by the vain drinking of healths," which practice is straightway forbidden. Excess or bravery of apparel is condemned, and no one is to wear a dress "with any lace on it, silver, gold silk, or thread under the penalty of forfeiture." Again, it is provided that children or servants are not to have ornamental apparel. Here is an individual case. Robert Coles, in March 1634, for drunkenness is disfranchised and condemned for a whole year to "wear about his neck, and so to hang upon his outward garment a D made of red cloth and set upon white"—a very unromantic scarlet letter! These things, too, passed away, but in the Maine Liquor Law of 1851, one traces the revival of the old idea. In England the thing lived not again. Under the Commonwealth public opinion enforced a "sober garb." Charles II. had some idea of a national costume, but he was too wise or too careless to attempt legislation. In 1747 the wearing of the Highland dress was forbidden, but that was policy, just as centuries before the Jews had a special garb ordained for them. Also a number of laws were passed to promote home manufactures: so under Charles I. and Charles II. the entry of foreign bone-lace was prohibited, though the second monarch granted licence for importing same to John Eaton for the use of the royal family. It would also serve, he coolly remarked, for patterns. There is one other curious example. Too much foreign linen was used, and so the 30th of Charles II. c. 3 ordered the dead (save the plague-stricken) to be buried in woollen shrouds. The relatives must file an affidavit with the clergyman as to this, and £5 was the fine for *him* if he neglected his part. Did the vision of that unseemly shroud really disturb poor Nance Oldfield's last moments, as Pope would have us believe?

> "Odious! in woollen! 'twould a saint provoke!"
> Were the last words that poor Narcissa spoke.
> "No: let a charming chintz and Brussels lace
> Wrap my cold limbs and shade my lifeless face!"

"Narcissa" had her wish: the "Brussels lace" of her head-dress, her "Holland shift," a "pair of new kid gloves on her cold hands," were the talk of the town; so they tricked her out for Westminster Abbey.

Almost up to Waterloo the Act lingered on the Statute Book, till some ingenious rascal brought an action against various clergymen for the £5 penalty, for that they had not certified to churchwardens the cases of non-compliance. And so, in 1814, the 54th George III. c. 108 swept away the strange provision.